This book is dedicated to my dear friend Max who passed away in 2020 at the age of 13.

I wish you were here to share these adventures with me.

www.diaryofanautisticteenager.com

AUTHOR'S NOTE

Right, nice to meet you, my name's Tom. I'm certain you already gathered that information from the cover, but whatever. Thought I'd introduce myself otherwise you'd be in for a shock; I'm not like most people. No, I don't have superpowers, far from it actually. As I'm sure you could guess from the title, I'm autistic, so I honestly have no idea what you think you're getting yourself into. If you're easily offended by anything, maybe this isn't the book for you, but tough titties I guess because I'm assuming maybe you already bought it. Thank you for your money. Anyway, back to introducing myself. I'm a curly-haired idiot who has no idea what he's doing most of the time. Also, I go off on tangents on the most random topics, so you're in for a treat if you like that kind of thing. I dunno what else to say, so let's begin, I guess. Oh, and there are probably lots of typos in this book because I'm shit at typing and I can't be bothered to get rid of them, so you're just gonna have to deal with it. Cheers and sorry.

Tom

Tuesday 1st Feb 2022

Felt tired this morning but still in an oddly good mood. My dog had an erection when I gave him his biscuit this morning before I left for the bus.

At the bus stop the two other kids were being knob heads and kicking a big stick around. Felt bad for the other normal bloke who had to put up with their shit.

Found out it was Chinese New Year in form because we watched a video about it. It was about a bunch of animals who had to cross a river in order to be first in the calendar. I think it's a stupid story because the animals have the real-life characteristics of the animals like the pig being lazy and the rat being a prick, but none of them ate each other.

I don't know if the Chinese are actually stupid enough to believe that actually happened or if they just think it's a nice story. I wouldn't put it past them though because everything in China is stupid. Especially the food.

There is nothing I hate more than the idea of zodiac signs and pseudoscience. I read somewhere that one in three people believe in all that. Sounds about right, most people in my school are retarded.

Break and lunch are the worst. It's like the Travis Scott concert in there. People shoving about in a small, crammed area. One of the tall people taped a banana to the ceiling. I now have to avoid that area, so it doesn't fall on me.

My stomach has been bubbling all day, but no one wants to use the school toilets because apparently the locks don't work. I haven't set foot in there since Alvin took a shit in the urinal anyway.

I've got double history this afternoon which I'm not looking forward to because last history lesson everyone thought I was weird because I burst out laughing when Edward ate his book.

I don't know what lesson is more boring, maths or history. Last maths lesson was pretty funny though. I ended up shouting at a deaf girl. I didn't know she was deaf, I had to tap her on the shoulder in the end to get her attention.

My arms and legs have been aching all day because yesterday I did a lot of weightlifting and squats so that I could fit into my Spider-Man costume better. I'm now going to do workouts with my brother every day.

I'm looking forward to my 200 lollipops arriving from Amazon because I'm hungry. They're the same ones you'd get at the hairdresser when you were younger. Except I didn't have to go to the hairdresser 200 times. I am a genius.

I had a conversation with Luke about getting circumcised. Apparently, it takes ten days to heal, and he was telling me all about how he couldn't go ten days without a wank because of hot girls on TikTok.

Wednesday 2nd Feb 2022

I came up with a poem about a fat man who fell out of his kayak.

"The wealthy man was an unhealthy man, too wide to have a ride in his kayak.
It would wobble and shake, what a mistake was the fat man and his kayak.
The boat would capsize, for it's not wise for a fat man to own a kayak.
Everyone would laugh and stare because nothing could compare to a fat man rolling out of his kayak.
Waddling home sad and wet was the fat man who I bet went for a jog instead."

In art, the girl sitting next to me said *"there's no such thing as fat"*, she's clearly never been to America.

I came up with an invention. You know those scratch and sniff stickers you'd get as a kid? I thought maybe you could make pants like that. Like a new sex toy thing. I'd call them scratch and sniff underwear. Good for couples. They'd smell like strawberries. I guess they'd only be single use though because the smell would go when you wash them. You'd have to buy them in packs like nappies.

Turns out the girl in maths yesterday wasn't deaf, she just wasn't listening to anything I was saying.

Thursday 3rd Feb 2022
I saw two women at the bus stop today. They both looked like GTA prostitutes.

Had a conversation with Harry about one of those drive through zoos. He told me about a time a monkey ate bits of their car. I don't like those zoos; monkeys did the same thing to our car this one time.

Luke told me he had a glue stick in his trousers and told me to feel it. Turned out it wasn't a glue stick. Can't believe I fell for that.

Edward (the school idiot) told me he gets George Floyd mixed up with Guy Fawkes. He says he gets them mixed up because they have the same initials, GF. I think this is stupid because George Floyd didn't try to blow up parliament.

In SEN (the learning support place) there was a kid doing beatboxing. He wasn't very good.

Had an isolation today for forgetting to go round the one-way system due to COVID-19. Reminds me of the time I got an isolation in my old school and ended up eating all the deputy head's coffee sweeteners out of boredom. One of the boys in isolation was secretly on his phone. He was watching a sexy car wash video. I thought he was a bit weird.

A seagull shat on my knee when I was walking to science. I hate seagulls. That's the 2nd time in under a month that I've had a literal shitty encounter with one. I think they should piss off back to Brighton rather than trying to shit on me.

Told Edward that if he drinks the hydrochloric acid in science, he'd be alright if he wore his safety goggles. Thankfully he didn't actually do it. Turns out he's not that retarded.

I'm allowed to say the word *"retard"* because I'm autistic and it's like the n-word pass for morons.

Did a bit of research into scratch and sniff underwear to see if it's already been done and it turns out it is already a thing. I swear everything's a thing nowadays. I genuinely thought that was an original idea. Some knobhead had beat me to it. Maybe I'm just not cut out to be an inventor. I did see an even worse invention the other day though. Someone had made a wheelchair with pedals. How fucking stupid is that. Yeah, put pedals on a device made for people who can't use their legs. At least I'm not that dumb.

Friday 4th Feb 2022

Had an idea at the bus stop today. They should make a drink that tastes exactly like Calpol. That way I can drink as much Calpol as I want without dying. I think that'd be a genius idea because Calpol tastes amazing, especially the strawberry one, and no one wants to accidentally overdose.

This girl was showing me and my mates her sex videos she recorded with her boyfriend. There was this one video where she was giving him a blowjob and I got confused and said it looked like she was beatboxing. Everyone laughed at me.

In PSHE, Ted started barking at me like a dog. I wonder if he does that to his girlfriend. Wouldn't be surprised as they act like dogs together anyway; biting each other, sticking tongues in each other's mouths. Young couples are always weird and annoying. Why does my brother's girlfriend suck on his neck? He probably needs to wear a scarf in public now. I remember the time I got rejected by a lesbian. Glad that happened, young relationships are hassle.

A girl in class told me her spirit animal was a possum. She definitely looks like one. I honestly think she's almost as stupid as Edward.

I saw a very small teacher at break. Got told off for saying Warwick Davis was probably taller than her.

Edward brought in a pot plant today. He started eating it. He said he brought it in as a replacement for his mate who was ill today. Don't know why he ate it though. Now the idiot has mud in his bag.

We looked at the Boyle Family in art today. They made replicas of brick walls and paths. They didn't even try to do anything interesting with it. It was just a brick wall. I think modern art is stupid. People are running out of ideas and now anything is art. Watching paint dry used to be a saying for boring things, now it's probably an art exhibit. What a scam.

Saturday 5th Feb 2022

Felt taller this morning. Never realised how low down the toilet was.

Read on the internet that a dad had introduced a swear jar to his son who had Tourette's. thought that was funny.

A man walked past my house today who looked like Mr. Bean. Thought about writing another poem about it but I'm too lazy.

Don't think I'll do my diary on the weekends as I haven't got much going on. Half the day's already gone by the time I wake up anyway.

Monday 7th Feb 2022

Fell off the bus today because the steps were slippery. I looked like a right knob head.

Rob was showing me his stormtrooper keyring in form today. I said he must be a big Star Trek fan. I'm surprised I didn't get a smack in the face.

Saw a video of a guy who smoked so much he now speaks in autotune. He probably also has lung cancer. Made me think about all the chavs in my school like Mason and Nancy and how they'll probably end up like that.

I'm watching Edward try to play badminton as I write this. He didn't hit a single one. Felt kinda bad for him. Most of the time he just stood in the middle of the court and watched his teammate do all the work. He looked like he just didn't belong there.

Edward brought in an old thank you card that Rob had given him when he was a toddler. It had a photo attached to it of baby Rob. Turns out Rob and Edward grew up together, I didn't know that. The letter said *"To Edward, just a little note to say thank you for the Mr. Potato-Head you sent me. Lots of love Robbie."* I'm now going to call Rob Robbie for the rest of his life to piss him off. What I found really funny was the photo attached. Rob looked really ugly as a toddler. I guess all young children look like E.T. though.

Edward also brought in a small blue elephant watering can he found in a car park. We filled it with Radnor Fizz and Rob drank some. He probably now has AIDS.

Read my poem about the fat man in the kayak to my English teacher. She said she loved it and wanted a copy. I'd have to be careful though because I didn't want her showing it off to people and passing it off as her own. I might have to put a big water mark on it or something.

At lunch Edward was telling me about how all bald men come from Birmingham. Sounds about right.

Tuesday 8th Feb 2022

One of the boys at the bus stop was humping the bike rack today.

Rob did a thumb war with Nat in form. Rob pulled the forbidden method and sucked his thumb so she wouldn't want to win. Easy.

In English we had to sit in the hall and were given a lecture about the questions in the GCSEs. The sun was shining on the PowerPoint slide so we couldn't see anything. They tried closing the blinds to fix the issue, but they were slit blinds, so the sun was still coming through because of the angle. I don't see the point in those blinds, they only ever get half the job done. It's like if you put curtains through a shredder. Stupid. We could only see half the presentation because of the stupidly designed blinds.

A small hairy man walked through the hall during the lecture. I was bored and decided to write a poem about a small hairy man.

"Explorers looking for Bigfoot. Smallfoot's what I found.

Legs so shot and stubby, didn't go very far with a single bound.
Small hairy man walking along, like an Oompa Loompa he's singing a song.
He'll need more than a hair net to keep all that hair under control, so much hair it made him look like a troll.
Small hairy man enjoying his day, he's a funny looking bloke some might say."

After writing my kayak poem, all the girls have been asking me to write them a poem. Thought it'd be funny if I wrote some short hairy bloke a poem and not them.

At break Edward brought in an old, scratched FIFA 14 disc. We played frisbee with it. It ended up landing on the roof. We had to get Joseph (the small kid) to climb on Rob's shoulders to get it back.

A fat girl was blocking the corridor. Got told off for being late to my lesson.

At lunch we kicked around the FIFA 14 disc like it was a football. I think kicking the disc around is more fun than playing the actual game. It eventually smashed and the boys held a funeral for it.

Our history classroom is above the SEN department. We have to have the doors open to help circulate air because of Corona Virus. This meant we could hear all the noises the autistic people were making downstairs. There was this one autistic kid who was whistling the Star Wars theme the whole lesson.

Wednesday 9th Feb 2022

I pushed on a pull door this morning. I want to die.

Sat next to a girl with a broken leg in PE today. She said she'd rather do PE with a broken leg than sit next to me. The sad bit was they were playing football. Kinda hurt.

At break Edward pulled out a tin of SPAM. I said we should heat it up in a microwave. I thought it'd be funny if we heated it up in the tin. I'd forgot metal and microwaves don't mix. That's all I have to say about that.

Had my COVID vaccine today. Conveniently I was wearing a long sleeve shirt. Had to take off my top in front of all the girls so they could inject my shoulder. Lucky them. All those workouts I've been doing to look like Spider-Man finally paid off.

Told a funny joke in art about yogurt. Everyone laughed. I would write it down, but I can't remember it now.

Mark keeps sneezing in my hair. I tell him to do it in his elbow, but he doesn't listen. Now I'm glad I have the vaccine.

Spent my lunch break chasing seagulls. I didn't get shat on once.

Thursday 10th Feb 2022

Read an article about a baboon that escaped a research facility in Australia. Thought that was very interesting.

In skills, I set all the backgrounds on the computers to a photo of two monkeys fingering each other. I got sent outside.

Chris was telling me about how he scratched his girlfriend's mum's car with his wheelbarrow. What an idiot. If I'd done that I would have run away and never see her again.

I've got double maths today. I think Thursday is the day I look forward to the least. Nothing good ever happens on Thursdays.

A tall ginger guy was staring at me. He looked like if Post Malone didn't have all those tattoos. I felt really uncomfortable.

In maths someone had spilt monster munch on my chair. I'm now worried I'm going to be walking around with monster munch stuck to my arse.

A girl squeezed my arm in maths. I think she was trying to be friendly, but she squeezed where I had my injection. It really hurt.

In maths we were given a question about two shops. I think it was a percentage question to do with money. One of the shops was named Brian's Bonanza. I've never heard of a more stupid name for a supermarket. Maths questions are always so weird. It's always about some bloke buying 200 watermelons or something.

I look really weird walking around with my diary in my pocket. It looks like I have a giant rectangular erection. No wonder everyone keeps staring at me.

Sat on my balls in science. It really hurt.

Friday 11th Feb 2022

Nearly fell down the stairs and died this morning.

Saw a cross-eyed bloke at the bus stop today. Couldn't tell if he was looking at me or not.

Ted was making race car noises in form. He sounded like he was having a seizure. It got really annoying very fast.

We did a world map quiz in form. I noticed that Africa looks just like a bigger version of South America. Thought that was interesting.

I also learned that red pandas aren't actually pandas or even bears. Makes sense, they look more like racoons.

I could see Mark's arse crack in form. Reminded me of when a plumber comes round your house and bends down to fix your sink.

Rob was picking his nose in history. I joked and said it looked yummy. He thought I was weird.

At break, Edward brought in a very long wooden spoon used for making jam and a Christmas vinyl record. It was The Meaning Of Christmas by Boris Gardiner. He wanted to play bat and ball with them using the spoon as the bat and the record as the ball. He tried scratching the record with a pen to see if it would play. This internally hurt me because I collect records. I ended up stealing it so that he couldn't smash it to bits. I said instead of bringing in stuff to smash, he should try bringing in something like some eggs and spoons so we can do an egg and spoon race or something.

A girl said she was having trouble reading. She said she needed glasses. I told her that her glasses were on her head. She said they were fake glasses. I think it's stupid that she needs glasses but wears fake ones.

I sat in glue in science, now I have white stuff on my bum. I now look even more like an idiot.

It's Friday, that means it's chip day. That also means the seagulls are out and about. Thought I should go hide in the boy's toilets but quickly found a bunch of chavs smoking in there. Went and sat in the canteen instead.

They found out I stole the vinyl. They now want it back. They're not having it back.

The fat kid started breakdancing at lunch. Looked like if you dropped a big piece of jelly on the floor.

In art I had to comfort a girl because she broke up with her boyfriend. I'm very good at making people laugh. When I say that, I mean I'm very good at letting people make fun of me. However, I am told I am very good at comforting people.

Monday 14th Feb 2022

It's Valentine's Day today. Not gonna lie, I'm quite jealous of all the couples. To me I guess relationships are like a Lamborghini. You would like one but can't get one and if you could get one you wouldn't know what to do with it. They're also very expensive to keep.

It's a wet and rainy day so all the worms were out and about. They were all squished on the path. I must have seen at least eight of them while walking to the bus stop. Reminded me of a fact I learned over the weekend. Foreskin is actually a good replacement for eyelids so if I ever lose my eyelids, I can use my foreskin as a replacement. I now want to keep my foreskin in case I do lose my eyelids because I don't want some other bloke's foreskin on my eyes.

At break Edward brought in a half drank carton of apple juice and an old Lego Batman game. Apparently, the game is broken and whenever he starts it, it only plays the intro and not the game. I'm concerned he just forgets to press the start button and that the game isn't actually broken. For some reason the apple juice carton is all in German. There's not a single word of English on there. It also goes off in 8 months. I think there's more preservatives than apple juice in that carton.

I wonder if girls ask guys to be their Valentine. Hasn't happened to me yet. Don't want to get my hopes up. Joseph asked me to be his, but I don't think that counts because he's not gay and he already asked 14 other guys the same thing.

A girl commented on how curly my hair was. She asked if I had a Valentine and I said I didn't. She then made a weird noise. That's nothing special though. She has shit taste in guys. Her last boyfriend cheated on her. She's not my type either.

My watch kept making an annoying beeping noise in English. I yelled at it and called it a fat prick. I got told off. I hate those watches that count your steps. I keep tapping on things because I have autism and it thinks I'm running a marathon.

At lunch Rob said he'd suck Darron's knob for a swig of his Pepsi. It truly is Valentine's Day.

No one asked me to be their Valentine in the end. I guess it is a stupid tradition anyway.

Tuesday 15th Feb 2022

Found out my mate Martin got a girlfriend yesterday. Mother fucker looks like Jabba the Hutt and still gets more bitches than me. She's not an ugly one either, but he looks like a walking crisp packet and still managed to get her. To be fair though, I did give him some advice, so I'll take some credit. But still. Ridiculous!

Thought I'd listen to some Christmas music to cheer myself up. Nothing gets you in a good mood quite like Christmas music, unless you're one of those knob heads who hates Christmas music. If that is you, you can get in the bin.

In form we played a game of pin the tail on the donkey. Grace had to spin Josh around. I wish I was Josh, she's quite attractive.

In English, Joseph was making fun of Welsh people. He said they wake up and put their dick in a sheep.

We had to stand up and walk to the front to get sheets. I told Joseph I couldn't because I had an erection. It was one of those that just come out of nowhere. I told Joseph to go up and get mine for me. He said he couldn't because he was having the same issue. We couldn't do the hands in pockets strategy because we needed our hands free to carry the things, so we got someone from a different table to get them for us.

Edward had brought in a skull he had found. I can't tell what animal it belonged to. Probably a bird or a fox or something like that. I didn't want to touch it because I didn't want a disease. Edward was analyzing the skull. He said it has a really long nose and therefore must be a Jew. He really is autistic.

I kept getting bumped into at break. Felt like I was playing bumper cars. People really don't seem to care.

In skills, the girl who showed me her nudes started doing the worm dance. To be honest with you, she only did this because I told her to because I'm running out of things to write. She then started telling me about her favorite condom flavours. I asked if she liked the strawberry ones and she said she didn't. She does like the blueberry ones though.

Harry told me about the time he put his dick in a Henry Hoover. I think I need some new friends.

At lunch I found out that most fat people aren't jolly, but miserable. You learn a lot talking to different types of people. For example, a Welsh guy confirmed what Joseph had told me earlier. I'm now quite concerned.

Rob and Joseph were talking about what would have happened if Keanu Reeves wasn't good at swallowing pills in the movie The Matrix. They said it would have been a great time to stick in an advertisement for Buxton water bottles to help him swallow it. I don't think it would have made the movie any better.

In history Edward was talking to Rob about what he does in his free time. Rob asked Edward if he uses Discord, Edward said he doesn't. In his free time, he looks at his walls. He says they are nice looking walls. He also stares at the bumps on his ceiling and tries to find constellations. To be fair to him though, I used to try and find faces in the marble pattern on my bathroom floor so that's not very odd to me

Wednesday 16th Feb 2022

Yesterday my brother saw my bulge in my Spider-Man costume and said I need a bigger penis. What a knob head.

In form I talked to my mates about what they would do if they loved a girl and then found out she had a penis. Ted said he would stop being interested in her. I said I wouldn't mind because I'm already in love with her. If I knew she had a penis in the first place I probably wouldn't have gotten interested, but now that I am, I wouldn't mind. They called me gay. This annoyed me because I don't think I am.

While getting changed for PE, Rob started talking about how whenever he needs a piss, he can feel it in the end of his knob. I have no idea what he was talking about and neither did any of the other boys. We suggested he go see a doctor or google it.

A guy walked past me in PE. His hair literally looked like if you spilled macaroni and cheese on his head. He looked ridiculous. At least my curly hair looks nice, his makes him look weirder.

In art we were watching a fat bloke walk around.

We went for a walk round school to take pictures of the floor for our texture project. I hate modern art.

I had an itchy foot, so I had to do that thing where you stomp the ground awkwardly to get rid of it.

Saw a tree that looked like it had herpes. I took a picture of it.

I noticed I had bird poo on my shoe. That annoyed me.

A girl said she wanted me to splash in a puddle for her photo. I ended up with wet mud all over my legs and bum. I looked like an idiot. She didn't even take the photo in the end because she forgot to press the button. It was kinda fun though.

It now feels really uncomfortable to sit down because of my wet trousers. I did try to dry them with paper towels but that only got rid of the mud and not the water. It also made it into my shoes so I'm now squelching around. I now know not to jump in puddles unless I'm wearing boots.

Saw a guy who looked really weird at lunch. Couldn't tell if he had a really small top lip or big teeth. I think it's both. He looked like Freddie Mercury. He also had a really big bottom lip to make his top lip look ever weirder.

Some girl kept taking photos of me. She then gave the phone to her friend and told her to take photos of her with me. I felt like a celebrity. I looked like one too in the sense that I looked really awkward and didn't know why I was being photographed. She probably now has more photos of me than my mum does.

Some chav was blocking the one-way system because he was mucking about and pushing around with his mates. I got told off for being 5 minutes late to maths.

My friend told me about the time he donated £1 of his mate's money to a charity box. His mate wanted the £1 back so they took the money from the charity box. Seems pointless to me. Not much you can get with £1, so might as well donate it to charity.

I sat on my balls again in science. I swear I did the same thing at the exact same time last week. I need to learn how to not do that.

Thursday 17th Feb 2022

Had a bad dream last night. I dreamt my brother wouldn't let me come in the kitchen because he was having sex with two girls in there. This upset me because I wanted a bagel. I told him to piss off and do it in his room because other people want to use the kitchen. One of the girls was sitting on the bar stool waiting for her turn. I don't think that's how a threesome works. For some reason, their dads were sitting there and watching as well. Thought it was silly they were allowed in to watch, but I can't make my bagel. I woke up in a bad mood because I never got my bagel.

Thought I'd try to be kind this morning despite my bad mood. I let a year 7 girl sit next to me on the bus because I thought doing some good would make me less annoyed. When we had to get off the bus, she let everyone else get off the bus before us. This meant I had to wait for literally everyone else to get off the bus before I could because she wasn't letting me. Now I'm in even more of a bad mood because of stupid year 7s.

In form the boys did a competition against the girls. We had to beat them at chucking paper balls in a bin. We absolutely shit on them. This is what winning feels like.

Saw a girl wearing a shit load of makeup. She looked like a clown. She also had drawn on eyebrows. She looked stupid. I imagine when she goes home, she has to scrape it all off with her fingernails in thick clumps. It'd take a lot to get rid of all that. It looked more like face paint than makeup.

In skills the sun was shining in my eyes. I tried closing the blinds, but because we need the windows open due to COVID, the wind kept blowing the blinds forwards so that the sun could continue to blind me. When the wind did eventually suck the blinds closed, Harry pulled it back so he could blind me. Knob head.

Harry called me weird for being annoyed about not getting a bagel in a dream. He says that out of all the things to be angry about, I'm angry about not getting a bagel that doesn't even exist. It seemed pretty real at the time.

A pretty girl walked past me. I tried to breathe in to see what she smelled like. Nothing special.

At break Joseph told me he likes hairy balls dipped in chocolate. Whatever that means. Sounds kinda gay to me.

Edward had brought in some sort of puzzle box you need a key to open. He had lost the key. We tried to pick the lock. Rob said he had maxed out his lockpicking skills in Skyrim but when he tried to pick the lock, he got the wire stuck.

Again, I was late to maths because I was faffing about with the box.

In maths, Rayan sat in glue that was on his chair. He looked stupid. Glad to see it happen to someone else this time.

Michael was trying to be funny. It didn't work. He tries too hard to be funny. When you do that, the joke doesn't work. Michael says something once and no one laughs. When no one laughs, he assumes no one heard it so he says it again. Turns out we did hear him, and he just isn't funny. I don't like Michael. He's also the type of person who laughs at his own joke when no one else is. Knob head.

Rayan is an idiot. He said Singapore was the capital of Greece.

Gen accidentally called the teacher Mum. I had a great time making fun of her.

At lunch we gave up on trying to pick the lock on the box and just smashed it open on a bike rack. The box had nothing in it.

Some gay kid keeps squeezing my muscles. I can't be bothered to tell him to piss off.

Friday 18th Feb 2022

Today was a really windy day. Storm Eunice was being a knob head and breaking a bunch of shit. I got up, had a shower, brushed my teeth, got dressed, and walked to the bus stop. I then got a text message saying school was closed due to the dangerous storm. While walking back I noticed there were practically no cars on the road.

I was sitting in my room when the power turned off. Turned out a big tree had fallen on the power lines on my road. This means I can't use anything electronic for a while. No oven, no stove, no microwave, no fridge, no hot water, no heating. We also have no water at all because it's pumped from the bottom of the garden which takes electricity. This makes taking a shit very difficult because you can't flush the toilet.

Things were alright in the day, but when it got later, we had to carry around torches and put candles around the house. If the house burns down, I'm gonna be pissed off.

My dog is quite excited. He keeps humping my little brother. This is odd behavior because we had his balls removed. I think that's supposed to make him less... you know.

I'm getting very agitated because I need a piss. I'm also fucking freezing.

Because we can't cook anything and everything in the fridge is now warm, we decided to go to a restaurant for food. While driving there, I noticed there was a bunch of branches in the road. We had to keep swerving to avoid them.

We then walked from the car park to the restaurant. I don't think it was a good idea to wear a Hawaiian shirt in the worst storm the UK has had in three decades. On the way from the car park to the restaurant, I saw a bloke who looked exactly like Stephen Merchant. Height and all. Don't think it was him though.

I hate going to restaurants and public places. I'm always scared I'll see someone I recognise or vice versa. Not much you can do in those situations. The last time that happened was in Waitrose. I recognised a girl I knew, and she recognised me. She tried to ignore me, which is pretty reasonable. Unlike what I did, which was to call her name across the aisle and run up to her and give her a high five.

I thought I saw her again at the restaurant. Turned out it wasn't her; she isn't Asian. To be fair though, she did look exactly like her if she was Asian.

There is a bloke with really dirty hair sitting opposite us. Kinda put me off my food.

I had steak and chips. It was really good. I usually don't like steak because it gets stuck in my teeth. This time was no exception, but the chips were nice.

The house was freezing when we got back. So were my hands. I went on TikTok because there was no TV to watch. Saw a video promoting testicular cancer awareness. Thought I'd check my balls for cancer. It really hurt because my hands were cold. I guess I'd rather have cold balls than cancer though.

I spent the rest of the day in a cold, dark house. Miserable.

Saturday 19th Feb 2022

Apparently, they won't get the power back for a while. This means I can't have a shower for ages. I feel like that guy with dirty hair in the restaurant yesterday.

Dad bought a camping stove and a propane tank so we can have a cup of tea. It's also because my mum was complaining she can't have warm water to wash her face because she's going to a wedding today.

I have homework set online due tomorrow, but I can't do it because I don't want to waste the battery on my phone. I'll go mad if I can't listen to my music.

We went to the Oxford M40 services to get a KFC because of the oven not working. There was an advert for a vegan sweet chilli dip. It comes with a chicken meal. Don't see the point in advertising something as vegan if it comes with chicken.

There is an ugly bald man sitting in front of me. He looks like if Charlie Brown grew up and became a drug addict.

My little sister is complaining that her ice cream is too cold. I told her to put it to the roof of her mouth for a laugh. She got a brain freeze.

There is a pretty girl in the line for Ben and Jerry's. She has an ugly jawline though. She looks nice from the front, but from the side she looks like a T-Rex.

My little sister has noticed me writing my diary. She thought she'd start her own. She copied what I wrote about me making her get a brain freeze, but she spelt KFC wrong. She spelled it "*CfS*". She even put a lowercase f. No idea how you can get it that wrong.

I'm now in a bad mood because I accidentally screenshotted my home screen when trying to turn my phone off. It's one of those things everyone does, and everyone hates. It's like stubbing your toe.

Sunday 20th Feb 2022

Saw a video of how bad the storm is by the sea. I hope all the seagulls die. That's what they get for shitting on me every day. Don't even know what they're doing over here anyway. We live nowhere near the sea. Pack it in seagulls, go home.

Saw the electricians walking down the road. I felt so relieved. I hate not being able to... well... do anything really. We rely on electricity nowadays.

Finally, the power got switched back on. The first thing I did was go and have a warm shower. I never realised how cold my feet were until I felt warm water. When I got out the shower, it felt like I had just stepped into Antarctica. The water had warmed up, but the house hadn't.

When I opened the freezer, a bunch of water came spilling out because the ice had melted. We have the freezer positioned next to where my mum does the ironing, so all the piles of clothes on the floor got soaked.

All the ice-lollies were melted as well. They weren't fully melted though, so we put them in a cup and had a slushie.

All the clothes that were left in the washing machine are now mouldy. They never got dried, so I guess that's what happens when you leave something in a warm and damp place.

Mum called me a retard because I was making weird noises.

I wonder if my diary will ever get famous like Anne Frank's or something like that. I reckon my life is pretty interesting. I think it would make a pretty good TV show. I'll kill myself if they put a laughter track to it though. I hate it when they do that.

Monday 21st Feb 2022

It's half term now, so I don't have school for an entire week. Great, nothing going on for seven days. I'm being sarcastic by the way. It's hard to be sarcastic if you're writing it.

Don't think I'll continue to do the diary over half term, nothing much to write about.

Thought I'd write a poem about the storm.

"Bins flying around because Storm Eunice gave them wings.
Saw a trampoline up there too, held together with springs.
My trampoline didn't fly off though because it's cemented to the ground.
Gypsies stole our last one, it was nowhere to be found.
Storm Eunice is knocking over trees.
Thought I recognised a girl at a restaurant, turned out she was Japanese.
Better watch out, Storm Eunice is about."

I think I can now call myself a poet.

Tuesday 22nd Feb 2022

I've changed my mind about what I said yesterday. I can't go a whole week without writing anything. I think I'll try to write a poem everyday about things I see or interest me. I've had nothing but compliments about my poems so far, so I suppose I should write more. I guess it's better than writing nothing.

I had a dream last night about a fat bloke who ate all my cheese and onion crisps. I think I'll write a poem about that.

> *"Fat man coming to ruin my day, to steal my cheese and onion crisps and take them away.*
> *Of course he steals the crisps, not something healthy like a cabbage.*
> *A bloke so fat like him, a healthy diet he cannot manage.*
> *Does he not realise stealing is a crime?*
> *Especially since those cheese and onion crisps were mine!*
> *Piss off back home fat man.*
> *Back home to eat more marzipan.*
> *Go have a jog you fat old prick, rather than eating a whole picnic.*
> *Fat man gone home after ruining my day.*
> *I feel rather sad, might watch a movie on Blu-ray."*

Don't know why I was so upset about having my crisps stolen in the dream. I don't even like cheese and onion crisps all that much. They give you shit breath as well.

I wonder if any pretty girls have ever had a dream about me. I don't mean a dream where I'm a shitty background character, I mean one where I'm a proper main character. I hope they have.

They say dreams have a sort of hidden meaning. I know that's a load of bollocks. Not only because I just googled it, but because some fat bloke stealing my crisps and my brother having sex in the kitchen can't mean anything special. I wonder if any English teachers out there will find a hidden meaning; they're always finding hidden meanings in shit that doesn't fully make sense.

Don't know what I'll write my poem about tomorrow. I think I'll go for a walk or something to have a look around to find interesting things. There's a lot of weird old people in my local area. There must be something.

Today I learned why 69 is a funny number. I don't want to talk about it.

I've always thought people are weird. I don't see the point in most of the things we feel and do. I often find myself feeling like shit about the most insignificant things. Even when I acknowledge it's silly, it still seems like a big deal. Just like that bagel or some pretty girl. My English teacher told me I'm a good thinker. Don't know where she got that from, I remember having a conversation with her about how big Hitler's penis was. Apparently it was very small. Of course it was.

Don't think I can be bothered to write for the rest of the day. I think I might go and have some crisps and a cup of tea.

Wednesday 23rd Feb 2022
Went for a walk through the local village today for poem ideas. Saw a cross-eyed bloke walking a really small ugly dog. I think it was the same bloke I saw at the bus stop that one

time. I wonder how he can see where he's going. Whenever I cross my eyes, everything goes double. My mum told me if I keep them crossed, I'll damage my eyes. If that's true, I'm surprised he isn't blind. Anyway, I wrote a poem about him. No offence to cross-eyed people by the way.

"Cross-eyed man walking to the shop, pretty sure he's the same bloke from the bus stop.
Must be weird to have a conversation with a cross-eyed bloke, I wouldn't stop laughing; they're funny looking folk.
Probably struggling to look where he's going, he might walk into a road without knowing.
Cross-eyed man walking his dog who was yapping at birds.
He was also reading a newspaper; don't know how he could see the words.
He was a normal-looking guy.
That was until you look him in the eye."

I decided to walk to the park to note down some things I thought might be poem worthy. I saw a middle-aged man watching some girls on the swings. I don't think he was their dad because the girls then started calling to their dad who was on the other side of the park. I am very suspicious he is a paedophile. He looks like one. He even has that moustache all paedophiles seem to have. I think I'll write tomorrow's poem about him.

A small dog ran up to me and dropped a ball at my feet. I threw the ball for it. I think that made my day.

I didn't really see much else and I was getting cold, so I decided to walk back.

While walking back, I saw two small people walking towards me. At first, I thought they were children, but as they got closer I realised they were old people. I wonder if people get smaller as they get older, or if people just used to be really small back in the olden days. It would make sense if they were. My house is really old and therefore has really low ceilings. It would be a pretty good explanation for why they didn't need high ceilings, because they wouldn't keep banging their heads, unlike us. All because they're shorter. Or maybe people just used to be shit at construction.

Saw a ladybird in my room. I let it crawl on my hand and I put it outside. I think it was the same ladybird that I thought was dead on my floor for about a week. I guess it wasn't dead and might have just been stuck in my carpet.

Thursday 24th Feb 2022

I wrote a poem about that nonce I saw at the park yesterday.

"Nonce in a playground looking at kids, I think he might touch them heaven forbids.
Birdwatching is what he says the binoculars are for.
I bet the next day police come knocking on his door.
He lives in his mum's basement and watches TV all day.
When he's out and about, keep your kids away.
He's turned to kids because he sucks with all the ladies.
He drives a white van made by Mercedes.
Jenny, Benny, Bert and Tim go running to Mummy in fear of him.
Put him in prison and lock the door, we can't have him touching kids anymore."

There is a good chance he wasn't actually a paedophile and I've just made a poem making fun of some random bloke. Then again, I guess that's the same as all my poems.

I've always wanted to write a poem for a pretty girl. Don't think I'd be very good at it though because none of my poems are very flattering. It'd probably earn me a slap rather than a kiss. Even if I did do a good job with it, it probably wouldn't work anyway. Don't think poems are in fashion anymore.

I don't think I'll go for another walk today because it's raining.

Friday 25th Feb 2022

I did practically nothing today. I went to the shop to get milk and walked to the park. The nonce wasn't there.

I was sitting on the park bench when a hot goth girl came and sat next to me. I said she looked like she came out of a Tim Burton movie. She got up and walked off. I never got her phone number.

I can't be bothered to write a poem. I haven't got anything interesting happening. I might come back to it later.

Monday 28th Feb 2022

Had a dream last night about a girl who showed me her boobs. I'm quite disappointed I woke up from that dream. That was the only good dream I've had in ages.

My mum says I need to eat more fruit and vegetables. Yesterday I had a packet of Haribo with natural fruit juices. If that doesn't count, I don't know why they bother putting it on the wrapper.

Amazon keeps recommending me life size cardboard cut-outs of Warwick Davis. It knows me well. Either that or it recommends everyone else the same things. He was much cheaper than all the other life size cut-outs. Probably because he's much shorter. I remember in primary school; my teacher was telling me about her sister with dwarfism. She said it was really sad because she couldn't reach the pedals in her car.

I feel really bad for people with dwarfism. I remember going to Universal Studios when I was younger and only being allowed on The Cat in the Hat Ride because I was too small for most of the others. That's probably what it's like for them, but worse because of bullying and all that.

Now that I think about it, I probably only went on The Cat in the Hat Ride because I was too scared to go on the others.

While walking to the bus stop, I was thinking about what I'd do if it were my last day on Earth. I think I might want to go to Cadbury World. I haven't been there in a while and I remember it being fun. I also remember them giving out free samples of chocolate. I think the last time I went there was on a school trip.

I have prom coming up relatively soon. I was wondering if I should ask anyone to be my date. All the pretty girls either aren't going, have already got a date, or aren't interested. I think I might just sit with my mates and have a dance with them instead.

The adapter thing I use to plug my headphones into my phone keeps breaking. I'm quite disappointed because they were advertised as being *"unbreakable"*. I was suspicious anyway because they came in boxes of two.

I saw a pretty looking stone on the floor while waiting for the bus. I picked it up and put it in my pocket. It was sharp though, so it kept digging into my leg on the bus. I wanted to show it to my mates, but I didn't want to carry it around so I put it on the floor.

In PE, I had to look after the disabled kid. When I say look after, I mean listen to him talk about Ben 10 for about 50 minutes.

It was raining outside. I kept thinking I was being shat on by seagulls but turns out it was just raining. I think I have some sort of PTSD from being shat on so many times.

My stomach made a weird noise in maths. Luckily, the kid sitting next to me can barely speak English. This meant I could just say it was him and there wasn't much he could do about it.

At break, Edward brought in some of his birthday presents to show us. When I say show us, I mean for us to piss about with. He had brought in another copy of FIFA 14 and some barbecue sauce. Dunno why he brought in barbecue sauce, but the last time he brought in FIFA 14 we kicked it around and played frisbee with it. It looked like he had bought it from a charity shop. It still had the sticker on it saying £1.

In English, the fat kid sitting next to me farted. It smelled like fudge.

At lunch, someone let off a stink bomb in the canteen. I was scared I'd shat myself and not noticed. They had to evacuate the canteen because of the smell.

We decided to play a game of frisbee with the FIFA 14 disc again. We then filled the case it came in with barbecue sauce. We put the disc in the case and handed it into reception. There is an evil receptionist, so it was very satisfying to hand in a FIFA 14 case covered in barbecue sauce. I imagine what her reaction was when she opened it.

My hands smelled like barbecue sauce for the rest of the day.

Tuesday 1st Mar 2022

I found a lucky penny at the bus stop today. I don't believe in luck, but it made me happy.

I'm quite tired because I was up late last night practicing my dance moves. Prom is about 2 or 3 months away and I want to impress all the girls.

I need to get a haircut because my hair is absolutely mad. I have thick curly hair, so if I don't get it cut for a while it turns into a sort of afro.

Martin messaged me. He's the one who looks like Jabba the Hutt by the way. Apparently, the girl he's dating sat on his

lap. LUCKY MOTHERFUCKER! Honestly! The things I would c
for a hot girl to sit on my lap. Maybe in college. Good for him
though I guess.

There was an old lady smoking at the bus stop. She kept
coughing. I did that thing where you would hold your breath
around people smoking so you don't get lung cancer.

It's pancake day today. We did a pancake race. I came last.

I tripped and fell over while walking to English. I don't think
I'll ever get a girl to sit on my lap at this rate.

In English, the teacher said I shouldn't have sex because I
shouldn't reproduce. I said, *"I'm going to have loads of sex
when I'm older."* Everyone heard me.

At break, Edward had brought in a list of all the things he
likes and dislikes. I copied them out.

Likes	Dislikes
- Space Jam	- New Top Gear
- Food	- Backwash
- BBQ sauce	- My sister
- Jam spoon	- Space Jam 2
- Candle wax	- The gay man
- Liquid candle wax	- New girl
- Yankee candle	- The word chimney
- The phrase "*like a razor blade on a cat wheel*"	- Glitter Force
- Planes	- MHA
- Murderers	- Funerals
- Old Top Gear	- Weddings
- Ball pits	- Rob talking about some stupid fucking podcast
- Pinball machines	- Art
- Stuff I find on the floor	- The people that closed down Atomic Pizza
- Pizza	- People who murder murderers.
- Atomic Pizza	
- Me	
- Dogs	
- My dog	
- Bowling	

I think that should give you a good idea as to what Edward's like. I don't understand why he wrote a lot of that stuff down. Don't know why he likes murderers, seems a bit weird. I can understand hating weddings and all that though because they're boring.

At lunch, Edward brought in his pudding spoon. He uses the exact same spoon to eat all of his puddings. He also never washes it. I said we should put it in the toilet, but he wouldn't let me.

Grace looks grumpy. I don't know why. I'm shit at reading people.

Rob bench pressed Edward. I was very impressed.

Wednesday 2nd Mar 2022

I saw a dildo in the bin at the bus stop. I think it was used. You wouldn't buy a dildo just to not use it and then put it in the bin. I think it might have belonged to someone staying at the inn at the end of my road. I once saw an empty dildo box on my road, so this isn't anything new.

I got shat on by a bird while walking to PE. It was all over the front of my jumper, my trousers, and a bit in my hair. It didn't shit directly onto me, it shat in front of me and the wind blew it into me. They say it's good luck to be shat on by a bird, don't see how that's lucky. I was walking in a group and I was the only one to get hit by it. I would think you'd want to be the only one to not hit by it, so it's hardly like finding a 4-leaf clover. I must be the luckiest person on the Earth if that is the case. Why do they always go for me? I had to wash it off in the sink when I got to PE.

I genuinely hate most of the birds in England. What is the point in most of them? Pigeons, seagulls, what do they do? They hardly contribute much to the food chain. All they do is steal our food. The last time I saw one being eaten was when my dog brought one in from the garden. They're useless to nature.

Sat next to a gay bloke in PE. I wonder if gay people get turned on by their own genitals. I think it would be less exciting to be gay. I see cock and bollocks in the mirror every morning, so it's not anything special to me. Gay people must get less excited by sex then. If a guy undressed in front of me, I wouldn't be as thrilled because I see it daily. If a girl undressed in front of me, I'd be way more excited because I don't see that very often. In tribes in the jungle, all the women have their tits out all the time and the men don't care because they see it every day. Probably the same with gay people. I asked the gay guy if he is turned on by his own genitals. He said he isn't. I don't understand.

In science, we made Alvin and the Chipmunk jokes to Alvin for obvious reasons. Alvin responded by saying he thought the female chipmunks were sexy and if he was a chipmunk, he'd... you know. I'm now concerned whether or not he has pets.

At break, Edward brought in a giant painting off of his wall from home. I tell him to bring in random shit from home so that I don't run out of things to write about, but I wasn't expecting him to bring in a giant painting from his living room wall. Everyone stared at us.

In art, Noah explained why I'm always getting shit on by birds. Apparently, my curly hair looks like a bird's nest from above. This means the birds are attracted to my hair and end up shitting on me. Nice to know.

In maths, the girl sitting behind me told me about a girl that was ignoring her. She seemed very angry about it. She then turned around and started talking to her friend. She told her to have sex with the boyfriend of the girl that was ignoring her. I thought that was a bit extreme.

The headmaster walked into the lesson to check how we were getting on. He said good morning. It's the afternoon.

Thursday 3rd Mar 2022

There was a spider on the toilet seat this morning. I went for a piss in the downstairs bathroom instead. I went back to it and smashes it with a tripod that I use for drum recordings. It fell on the floor and scuttled away. I hope it dies from blood loss. I don't even know if spiders have blood. I just googled it and it turns out they do. They also don't have bones, so the way they walk about is through blood flow in their legs or something. That means spiders are basically walking erections. It kind of comforts my arachnophobia to know that spiders are pretty much a more sophisticated version of my penis.

There was a guy eating a sandwich at the bus stop. The sandwich fell apart and the filling ended up on the floor. He looked sad, but the ants that went after it looked happy. I felt bad for him though.

In skills, Harry had a pen without the lid upside down in his breast pocket. The pen exploded and he got ink all over his nipple. He looked very silly.

I was watching Harry doing his business homework. He was working on a dog walking company called Waggies Walkies. That is the most stupid name for a company ever. Aside from Brian's Bonanza. I'm surprised I remembered that.

At break, Edward had brought in his daily bit of rubbish for me to write about. This time, I don't think it was rubbish and might actually be worth something. It was a Back To The Future cereal box. It was unopened. I reckon it might be worth a bit in the future because it's one of those collectable things. Back To The Future fans might go mental over that in like 30 years' time. Just like those old comics or those basketball cards or something. I wouldn't find it hard to believe people spending stupid amounts of money on an old cereal box with mouldy cereal inside. We told Edward not to open it just in case.

Edward invited me to his birthday party. I wasn't given a date or location, but I was told to write my name down on a piece of paper. Apparently it's bowling or something. I can't remember if I'm any good at bowling or not. Last time I went bowling I was too weak to lift the bowling balls, but since then I've been doing my workouts to look like Spider-Man. I'm quite happy I got invited to a party, I haven't been invited to one in ages. Probably because of the virus.

Mark's breath fucking stinks. I asked him if he brushed his teeth this morning and he said he didn't because he woke up late. It smells like it. My dog's breath smells better than his and they eat literal cow shit whenever we go for walks. I told him to put his face mask on.

I have double maths now. Great.

I saw a man having a tour of the school. He was walking around with his two daughters. The man looked exactly like Bill Murray. I love Bill Murray.

During maths, Emily went to go to the toilet. She wasn't looking where she was going and walked into the door.

The girl sitting behind me was chewing gum. When she tried to talk to me, the gum fell out of her mouth and onto the table. I laughed.

In science, we had a test. Alvin (the guy who shat in the urinal that one time) fell off his stool. It made a huge thud because he's very fat. I wonder what the people downstairs thought. They probably thought a bomb got dropped or something. It looked like he hit his head. I would be worried he has brain damage, but he can't get any more retarded, so I wouldn't be too concerned.

I told my mum about my day when I got home, and she said that I should never feel embarrassed because of all the idiots I see daily and how it can't be as bad as them. I disagree. The time I fell off the bus was embarrassing and so was the time I accidentally slammed my crush's fingers in a door.

Friday 4th Mar 2022

In form, we did a world book day quiz because it was world book day yesterday. Would have made more sense to do it yesterday. There was a question about a book called No One

Is Too Small to Make a Difference. We had to guess who wrote it. I said Warwick Davis. Turns out Greta Thunberg wrote it. I was disappointed because Warwick Davis is my favorite small person.

In PSHE, we went to the sports hall to play a game called kick mat rounders. No idea what that is. Sounds like the teacher just made it up. I think he's running out of ideas. He explained the rules to us. I think it's just normal rounders, except you kick a ball into a mat or something. I don't really know; I wasn't listening.

I'm not too keen on having a PE teacher as a form tutor because I hate sports. He is a lovely man though.

I keep catching Grace looking at me. Might be my imagination though. I want to ask her to be my date to prom, but I don't think she'll say yes. I don't even know if she's actually going or not. What I'm worried about is if I'll regret not asking her though. I'll think about it.

I know at the beginning of the diary I said I think young relationships are silly, and they are, but I think I'd like to have one. I said this on Valentine's Day, but I'm jealous of the people that do have one. I've only liked 2 people in my lifetime. The first, I slammed her fingers in a door and the other was already dating someone. Not a great success rate. I don't even know if I like Grace. I think she's pretty and all that, but I don't really know.

I don't react well to being rejected. The last time that happened, I did that thing salty guys do when they get rejected and try to make the girl feel bad. I don't think I ever ended up saying sorry. I wish I did. I still feel bad about it. I think I'd put that up on my list of most embarrassing things I've ever done. Up there with falling off the bus. I won't do it again.

In science, the annoying girl kept talking over the teacher. She looks like if Blackpool was a person.

At lunch, Edward ate a Babybel (One of those cheese things). He also ate the wax case it came in.

I read somewhere that if you stare at someone's forehead it makes them feel really uncomfortable. I tried it out on Joseph. I don't think it matters if you stare at their forehead or not. If you stare at anyone anywhere, you're going to make them uncomfortable. It probably isn't a matter of *"the forehead makes them more uncomfortable than if you stare anywhere else"*, because I can think of way more uncomfortable places to stare. Whoever came up with that is an idiot.

Monday 7th Mar 2022

People keep nagging me to write more poems. I don't think my last ones were very good. I think I need to wait for something truly poem worthy to happen rather than trying to force one. That's how all the best poems come about I think.

There was a woman standing at the bus stop opposite me this morning. She was wearing a wig. A big gust of wind came and blew the wig off her head. I had to turn my back and face a wall so that she couldn't see me laughing. I felt sorry for her though.

I keep getting sharp stabbing pains in my ears. I think it's because I'm constantly wearing headphones and listening to music on full blast. That'll probably do it. My brother says I look naked whenever I'm not wearing my headphones. I think I might go see a doctor about it because I think it's getting worse. If I go deaf, I'm gonna be pissed off because I want to be a musician.

There was a kid on the bus with what looked like toothpaste down his jumper. I can't believe he hasn't noticed. Maybe he has and just can't be bothered to wipe it off. Either way it really annoyed me.

For English homework we have been looking at articles. Read an article over the weekend about a mummified mermaid where if you eat bits of it, it grants you immortality. I wonder how they found that out. If I found a dead mermaid, I don't go *"I'll eat a bit of that"*. Turns out the bloke who found it was Asian, so no wonder he tried eating it. Have you seen some of the things they eat in Asia? Spiders, bats, chicken feet, any insect they find crawling about.

Thought the story about the mermaid was poem worthy, so I wrote a poem about it.

"Half fish, half woman.
Making sailors horny and Asian people hungry.
Mermaids are supposed to have lovely hair.
This one didn't, there was barely any there.
She might have looked nice when she was younger, didn't
stop that Asian man's hunger.
Being mummified for many years would do that to you, her
hair looked all dried up, get her some shampoo.

46

I wouldn't have a munch; I'd rather have a sandwich for lunch.
She looked like she tastes disgusting, mermaid flesh is not what I'm lusting."

There was shit on my seat on the bus. I'm worried I'm gonna have shit stuck to my arse for the entire day. I wouldn't be surprised if that were the case because that sort of thing would typically happen to me.

In maths, there was a girl singing. She sounded awful.

At break, Edward brought in a giant stress ball. I popped it. It had some sort of weird chemical inside it. It tasted disgusting.

Had a conversation with a girl about crystals. I said I don't believe in pseudoscience. She said she'd bring in some rose quartz. Apparently rose quartz makes people fall in love with you or something. I see this as a win-win. Either I get proven right, or I get a girlfriend. I'm worried it might backfire though. Most of the time I attract more men than women. I'm worried all the gay blokes are gonna be flocking after me and not the girls. That'd be annoying.

In English, we had to do a task where we describe a public swimming pool. I think it was some sort of exercise to test our describing skills. Anyway, I'll show you what I wrote. *"Public swimming pools: the public's sewers in disguise. Discarded plasters litter the place. Litres of urine take up almost as much of the pool as the water. Chlorine pickles your eyes. If you're unlucky enough to inhale some of the water, which you will, you have just tasted a concoction more deadly than George's Marvellous Medicine."* I'm pretty proud of that.

At lunch, I thought I saw a butterfly. Turns out it wasn't actually a butterfly, but a small piece of plastic floating about in the wind. I was disappointed.

In science, the girl sitting next to me sneezed. It really scared me.

Tuesday 8th Mar 2022

Last night I thought I'd have a go practicing more descriptive writing. I've got my GCSE coming up, so I want to be as good at it as possible. It's a good bit of revision.

I wrote two descriptions. One is a description of shops, and the other is about a traffic jam.

This is the one about shops. *"There is no place colder than the frozen aisle in a shop. Shops are cold, crowded, always have that rubbish music playing and are always out of stock in that one thing you came for. There's always that dilemma where you see someone you recognise. In those situations, you can either hide behind one of the displays, or say hi. Both are terrifying. Shopping trolleys are terrible. It's easier to jump on the back of a bull and not fall off than navigate a shopping trolly. The wheels on those things suck. Might be the reason I always see Tesco shopping trolleys in ditches and rivers. They always run away from you."*

Here's the one about traffic jams.

"There is no place on Earth more painful than a traffic jam. It's the sound of car horns yelling at each other as if that's gonna make the lights go green. It's a time more stressful than anything you've ever experienced. They only seem to happen when you're in a rush to get somewhere. After that, everyone's then in a bad mood because the traffic was bad. This means everyone starts being a dick to each other as a result. I imagine Satan invented traffic jams to annoy us and turn us insane. Sounds about right. Traffic jams are where dreams go to die."

You can probably notice I used the same starting to both of them. This is because I was running out of ideas for sentence starters. Aside from that though, I did a pretty good job of accurately describing them I think. I tried writing them about boring things to really test my writing capabilities. Turns out I'm a genius. I think I should write a book.

Apparently it's home clothes day on Friday. I wonder what Grace will wear.

We weren't allowed in the usual area at break. They were having exams in there, so we moved to the science block instead. One of the year 10s let off a stink bomb in science. They need to stop doing that. It smelled like egg. We went and stood outside in the cold instead.

In skills, my mate showed me this girl that he's been talking to. She looked alright.

Saw an unopened Wagon Wheel on the floor. It was still in the wrapper, but it was all broken up inside. Luke tried to make me not eat it by saying it was originally his and that he had rubbed his knob on it. I ate it anyway because I was hungry.

Some bloke was showing me his new coat. The zip was already broken.

I spent the rest of the lesson squishing the fat kid's boob. I reckon he has bigger boobs than all the girls in the year.

Oscar went to the toilet. He was in there for about 15 minutes. When he came back, he shouted "*I just took the fattest shit!*" I was surprised the teachers didn't really care.

At lunch, I asked Edward what he wants to be when he's older. He said he wants to be a librarian because he likes playing about with that red scanner thing they use to beep books when you take them out. He also says they just sit about on their arse all day and don't have to deal with much stress. Fair enough.

I bought Edward a birthday present. His party is next weekend.

Wednesday 9th Mar 2022

Thought I'd give Edward his present today because it's chocolate and I'd eat it if I didn't give it to him soon. I had run out of good wrapping paper, so I used some pink unicorn wrapping paper my mum had left over from my little sister's birthday. I don't know if Edward will be too pleased.

I had an awful dream last night. It was very anxiety inducing. It was about a woman who stepped on my foot and then chased me down to say sorry. I hate it when people do that. I'd rather we just forget it ever happened. Less embarrassing.

I have my mock GCSE exams next week. I'm not looking forward to them. The last time I had mock GCSE exams, I had a very runny nose. I had to use my face mask as a tissue and then wear it for the rest of the day. It kept sticking to my face and suffocating me. I guess that's what happens when you're too scared to ask for tissues. Also, some year 8s pulled the fire alarm while I was doing my English exam last time, so I hope that doesn't happen again.

There was an old man riding a bike on the road this morning. He was very slow. I reckon I could walk faster than him. He was holding up all the traffic. I think if you're that slow, you should cycle on the path instead.

I saw a guy sneeze. He got snot all over his face.

In form, we got bored and got out the maracas and bongos from the music department to play around with. Me and the boys formed a sort of band. It actually sounded alright. I wonder if Grace liked it. Apparently girls like it when boys play music for them. To be fair though, I wouldn't like it if they played music for me music with bongos in it. No one likes bongos.

I think I need to start eating breakfast in the morning. My stomach keeps making weird noises and it's quite embarrassing.

I'm still confused about if gay people get turned on by their own genitals. It's a question every straight person has asked at some point. Today I finally got the answer I was looking for. In PE, I asked the gay kid if I took a picture of his penis without him knowing, would he be turned on by it? I said he wouldn't know it was his because he wouldn't know I took the picture. He said he would probably still recognise it. I said I would pop it in Photoshop and change the lighting or something. He then said he would be turned on by it. I finally figured out how to make gay people turned on by their own genitals. I am a genius.

In art, the girl sitting next to me was listening to white noise sped up. Don't see how it could be sped up because it's just a flat sound. Maybe that meant it was just a shorter version of regular white noise because the song went quicker.

There is a girl sitting in front of me. She's definitely flirting with me. She was doing sex hand gestures to me and shit. She then asked me what I was thinking about. I said that my ear was hurting. She looked confused because that probably wasn't the answer she was looking for. I think I really need to see a doctor about it.

Edward liked the present I got him by the way. He wasn't too keen on the pink unicorn wrapping paper though.

Edward says he's never had a wank. I struggle to believe that. Everyone has. I tell him it's amazing, but he says it probably isn't as good as ice cream. I'm surprised he hasn't tried it. If not by urge, at least by curiosity. He says he doesn't want to try it because he says it looks painful. He's an idiot.

A pretty girl walked past my classroom in maths. She's the same girl I spent a whole history trip staring at. I haven't told you about her yet, but it doesn't really matter because I have no chance with her. When she walked past, I accidentally shouted *"She's pretty!"* I did this because I think out loud most of the time. This is probably why I'm shit with women because I'm always scaring them away. I hope she didn't hear me. I wonder how many things I've said about Grace that she's noticed. I just can't help myself sometimes.

Thursday 10th Mar 2022

I saw a slug chewing on a cigarette at the bus stop today. It made me think if slugs and things like that can get addicted to things. Maybe that slug goes round looking for cigarettes to chew on now because he's hooked. Doesn't seem too odd to me.

I remember when my mate and I were walking home from school and he found an unused cigarette on the floor. He went back to his house and got one of those lighters you use to light birthday cake candles. He lit the cigarette and smoked it to see what it was like. It only stayed lit for about 3 seconds because it was damp. I didn't smoke it because I was scared of lung cancer. We then chucked it in his fishpond for the fish to eat. Those fish are probably all dead now.

Our form room was temporarily changed because teachers were having a meeting in our usual one. It had been changed to the food room instead. We decided to set all the timers on the ovens to 2 hours and 25 mins. We wanted all the ovens to go off in the middle of a lesson for a laugh.

I asked Rob if slugs could get addicted to things like cigarettes and he said they most likely could. I asked him if I could keep a slug in a cage for a week and only feed it cigarettes. After the week, I'd switch it back to lettuce and see if it showed symptoms of withdrawal or something. I just think it'd be funny to watch a slug go mental. He said that if I fed it cigarettes for a week, it'd probably die. I googled if slugs could get addicted to things and the first thing that came up was talking about tobacco. Maybe slugs just love cigarettes. I don't know though because I couldn't be bothered to read it.

I had the EastEnders song stuck in my head for the entire skills lesson. I think that is possibly the most annoying song to have stuck in your head.

I stepped in yogurt while walking to maths. I was grumpy for the whole lesson.

Apparently, all girls have a sort of hand fetish. This means they all like veiny hands. I don't have very veiny hands, but I do have big hands. Girls must like that because it means I also have big fingers.

A girl offered to show me pictures of her boobs. I tried to be respectful and said no thank you. I regret saying that now. If a girl offers to show you her boobs, say yes. Don't make the same mistakes as me.

Friday 11th Mar 2022

Woke up to a text message from the gay kid I sit next to in PE. He had sent me pictures of naked men and was telling me all about them. I think he thinks I'm gay.

My piss was very yellow this morning. It looked like if you melted a Calippo and poured it into the toilet.

My little siblings keep shitting in the toilet and not flushing it. Maybe it's a good thing I don't have a girlfriend. If she ever comes to my house and wants to use the toilet and walks in on my brother's unflushed shit, she'd leave me and never come back. I think that's probably one of my biggest fears. Right up there with sharks and missing the bus.

It's home clothes day today. I was worried that I had got the dates mixed up while standing at the bus stop because the other kid was in normal uniform. Turns out he was the one who got the dates mixed up. Thank God. I would hate to be the only one in school wearing home clothes.

At school, I saw a bunch of people wearing designer clothes. I don't understand designer clothes. People only buy them for the brand, not because they actually look good. This results in them walking about and looking like an idiot. I saw this one bloke wearing a designer shirt that was just a white shirt with a logo on it. It looked like the type of shirt you'd find in a charity shop. You could get a white shirt from Primark and then get one of those iron on stickers and get the same result for a fraction of the price. That proves me right; they wear them for the brand, not the look. People who wear designer clothes are idiots.

A girl called me fit. She stank of sweat. I wasn't very flattered.

Grace looks lovely by the way.

I saw someone wearing a spiky dog collar. Call it a hunch, but I think they might be a My Chemical Romance fan. Every home clothes day, there's always those people that dress like retards.

We were supposed to bring in £1 for home clothes day to donate to Ukraine. Edward said he didn't have £1, so he brought in a £1 book token instead. What an idiot.

I keep getting compliments about my dress style. Everyone likes my Hawaiian shirt. Maybe that's why the sweaty girl called me fit.

One of the nerdy kids was wearing a turtleneck jumper. It made him look even more stupid. I hate turtlenecks.

All the girls were complaining they were cold. They were all wearing crop tops. I think they should check the weather before they wear crop tops on a rainy day. They didn't even bring a coat.

I think modern fashion is stupid. The girl's clothes look like they got pulled out of a bin. Ripped jeans and half a top. They just look broken. Boy's fashion isn't any more stupid. Most boys in my school wear adidas tracksuits all year round.

Saw a fat girl wearing a stripy top and trousers. She looked like a boiled sweet.

In art we had a cover teacher. The teacher put on music. I said, "Oh turn this off!" It was some sort of Egyptian music. They wouldn't let me put on any Led Zeppelin, so I had to sit and listen to something that sounded like it belonged in the Indiana Jones movie. My ears hurt now more than ever.

The teacher walked up to me to see how I was getting on. She smelled like one of those car air fresheners.

The girl sitting next to me said she thinks I'm a robot. I think it's because of my lack of social awareness. She should see Mark Zuckerberg. Everyone says he's a lizard.

I have a doctor appointment after school about my ears hurting. I went to go sign out at reception. The evil receptionist lady wouldn't let me go. I was annoyed because I was in a hurry and she was being a prick. I said, *"Oh fuckin hell."* She went mental. She eventually let me go. What a knobhead.

In the waiting room for the appointment, I saw a woman with her baby. The baby didn't look real. I thought it was a doll at first. It was very pale and looked like it was made of plastic. So did the mum. I don't know if that's the reason she took it to the doctors though. If my child looked like that, I'd be concerned. The thing is though, she also looked like that, so maybe it's just a family of ugly people.

A funny looking man walked out of one of the rooms. He looked like a goblin trying to be human.

It was finally my turn. The doctor said there was nothing wrong and that I have just been listening to too much music too loud. That's a relief.

Saturday 12th Mar 2022

My mum was doing ironing this morning. She was wondering why the iron wasn't doing anything. Turned out she hadn't turned it on.

Saw a video on YouTube about a guy who made a burger. He didn't put it in a bun. I didn't even know that was a thing.

Why would you have a burger without a bun? That's just like eating cereal with no milk. Some people do that though. Weirdos.

I had to pick up a bunch of sticks in the garden left over from the storm so that my dad could cut the grass. There was a lot of them. I got bird poo all over my hand. I had to put them all in the brown bin. The bin had soon filled up, so I started chucking the sticks over into the neighbor's garden. Don't think they'll be too happy.

Got pocket money today, so I spent it on sweets straight away. I got a bunch of gummy worms.

Went to see the new Batman movie today. It was good. It was also 3 hours long. By the time it had finished, I felt like I was going to piss myself. I don't like cinemas that much. You're always sat behind the tallest bloke in the world. You can never see anything. Some guy in front of me was on his phone for the first 15 minutes of the film. Knob head.

Stayed up late watching videos. Saw a video that was top 10 ghost sightings or something. All the comments in the comment section were saying "*I don't claim any negative energy*" and putting a bunch of crucifix emojis. Don't know why they bother doing that. What's that gonna do? It's not like the demon's gonna go have a look in the comment section and see they've typed that and go "*Fuck, guess I can't kill them*". If demons are real, they're absolutely useless. The most you ever see in those ghost videos is doors closing and shit falling over. If you come all the way from the pits of hell and all you can do is do exactly the same things the wind can do, what is the point?

I remember I bought a Ouija board because a bunch of people on my bus were saying about how they're dangerous and all that. I wanted to prove them wrong, so I bought one from eBay. I asked the ghost to possess me and rip my ball off or something and guess what happened. Literally nothing. The demon's probably still trying. Either that or he's lazy. Or not real.

I think I might bring my Ouija board into school and try and curse those crystal healing girls for a laugh.

Monday 14th Mar 2022

Told my mum she smelled nice this morning. She said I smelled like vomit. I don't think I want to go to school anymore. She was joking I think, but still.

Thought I saw the cross-eyed bloke at the bus stop again. Couldn't really tell because he was wearing sunglasses.

Saw my reflection in one of those plastic display cases when I got to school. My hair looked mental. It looks like one of those fancy-dress clown wigs minus the colours. I really need that haircut, but I can't be bothered. I kinda think it suits me though, so I guess it's not all that bad.

I saw a girl with a really big nose. They say if you have a big nose, you have a big penis. What if a girl has a big nose? Is there a female version? Like if she has a big nose, she also has big boobs or something. If a bloke has a big nose, they're ugly, but they have a big penis so it's not all bad. If a girl has a big nose, she's just ugly. No perks that come with it. Doesn't seem fair. Although, I did meet a guy who had a big ugly nose and a small penis. He also had a girlfriend. I have never been

59

so surprised in my life. He wasn't even that good of a person either. He was the type of bloke to spend his lunch break showing you pictures of cats on his phone. No idea how he pulled her. Sort of makes you think anything is possible.

I honestly have no idea how all these knob heads have girlfriends and I don't. To be fair though, their relationships only last about 4 months.

Apparently, it's world pi day today. The maths department was celebrating it. They had baked a bunch of pies. Hahahahahahaha, very funny maths department. They had left crumbs all over my chair and table. I was really annoyed.

I spoke to the crystal healing girl. She said she makes a wish every day at 11:11. I said my wish every day at 11:11 will be for her wish to not come true for a laugh. She got really angry at me. It was hilarious.

I accidentally upset Rob because I said chess is a board game. I have no idea why that upset him because it's true. It's a silly thing to get upset about too. If chess isn't a board game, what is it?

We've been doing revision in our lessons because we have mock exams all this week. I don't have any exams until Tuesday.

For English, we are looking at A Christmas Carol. I've been revising that in my lessons. I'm pretty sure I know it like the back of my hand. The Muppets A Christmas Carol used to be my favorite Christmas movie, so I'm pretty familiar.

I also have an English GCSE on poetry. I wish part of the poetry exam included writing a poem, I'd be very good at that. Unfortunately, it's just analysing poems that have already been written. I hate the education system, it sucks dick.

While sitting in English, I noticed a dead pigeon on the roof that the window overlooks. Good riddance, that'll be one less bird shitting on me.

I remember in an RS lesson this one time, a headless pigeon fell out of the sky and landed on a roof. It exploded in a puff of feathers and looked rather flat because it had been dropped from a height. I laughed at it, but my RS teacher got angry because she was vegan. I have no idea how that even happens. How does a pigeon lose its head mid-flight? My theory is either it had been partially eaten by a bird of prey and dropped from the sky or it got hit by a plane. Either way, it made the RS lesson funny.

Thought I'd write this week's poem about the headless pigeon that fell from the sky.

"Headless pigeon falling from the sky.
How that happened, we'll never know why.
It landed on the roof with a splat.
Falling from that height, it ended up flat.
Headless pigeon can no longer sing.
His head is gone, he can't do anything.
Poor little guy fell from the sky.
Without a head, he can no longer fly.
Some say aliens, I say a plane.
One less bird to shit on me, let's celebrate with champagne!

Headless pigeon on the roof top.
He's made a mess, grab a mop."

You can tell I'm running out of ideas at this point. My first poem was an absolute banger, but now I'm writing about shitty headless pigeons. How bad will it get? How little creativity will I have left? Next thing you know, I'll be writing a poem about some moss I found on the floor in a car park or something. Just some random shit only desperate people write about. People have been pressuring me to write a poem every week, so what do they expect?

Tuesday 15th Mar 2022

Today is the day my week starts to get shit. I've got exams. I have been doing revision, but it's still pretty nerve-racking. Today I got maths and English. Not that bad, I guess. I'm shit at maths and alright at English.

I was up late last night doing a bit of last-minute revision. I had to watch these maths videos on a website. The woman talking you through them is the worst at explaining things and she has the most annoying voice on Earth. If scientists tried engineered the most annoying voice possible, it would come nowhere close to that woman's voice. I got very frustrated with it. I think they should hire a comedian to do the talking on those videos, so you don't fall asleep halfway through or shout every swear word in the dictionary at your computer. The maths was annoying already, then they add that stupid voice to the equation. Knob heads. At least try and make it remotely fun or interesting. I ended up searching for a different tutorial on YouTube. I found some Indian bloke giving a way better tutorial.

I go to a separate room for exams because I have autism, so there's always a lot of confusion about where that place is. Everyone else has their exam in the sports hall, but I'm in some random room tucked away in the most unnoticeable place. The bad thing is they are always changing the room. The directions they give me are the worst. I always get lost. Finding the exam is more difficult than the exam itself.

The exam sucked. There were two Russian builders outside making a bunch of noise. You could hear them shouting the whole time.

I finished the exam with 30 minutes left. I attached my ruler to my pen, and it looked like a plane. The ruler being the wings and the pen being the body of the plane. Surely, I'm not the only person to have done that. Anyway, I spent the rest of the exam playing about with my imaginary plane.

When the person in charge of the exam went to the front of the room to say the exam had finished, they tripped and fell over. That was funny, so I guess the exam wasn't all that bad. When I stood up, the amount of bum sweat on my chair was insane.

Nothing else happened in the day. I don't think this week will be very interesting because it's just all exams and when it's not exams, it's silent revision.

Wednesday 16th Mar 2022

More exams. Brilliant. Not a very exciting week, is it?

The separate room I go to is where they send all the disabled kids. I'm not there on my own. This results in some...

63

interesting things happening in the exams. One of the disabled kids farted really loud in the middle of the exam. I genuinely think he shat himself.

After the exam had finished, I went to my science lesson. The girl sitting next to me said I'm lucky to be autistic. She said it means I get to park in the disabled parking spots. She's not wrong, but if that's the only good thing she can think about being autistic, maybe it isn't all that great. At least it makes me a natural genius... sometimes.

Thursday 17th Mar 2022

Literally fuck all is going on this week. I hate writing nothing. Just to fill space I thought I'd write another poem. I wrote a poem about some moss I saw on the floor in a car park. I know I used it as an example of what a bad poem would be, but I really am starved for ideas.

"Moss in a car park. Snails were eating it.
They were all in a huddle eating the moss in a puddle.
Moss in a car park, brown and green.
It's the mossiest moss I've ever seen.
It looked like it had been stepped on because it was all flat.
The bloke who stepped on it was probably really fat.
Moss in a car park next to some bird poo.
I stepped in that one, it was all over my shoe."

Would you believe me if I told you that took me 3 minutes to write?

The biology exam I had today was rubbish. Whoever put that paper together was a retard. The paper asked us to refer to a source we weren't given. It also asked us to explain our answer for a question that wasn't even included on the paper. That's not me being a retard and misreading the questions, everyone else had the same issue. I'm honestly surprised they don't read through the exams before they hand them out.

I just realised you can smell the inside of your nose. Thought that was weird.

At break, we put Jack's hair in a ponytail because he has long hair. He ended up looking like one of those gay music teachers.

In maths, the girl sitting behind me commented on how veiny my hands were. She was 100% flirting. I told you about how they all have some sort of hand fetish.

I have a drum lesson every Thursday after school. This week's lesson was cancelled because my dad has COVID. My drum teacher is quite odd. I wonder if he has hair. I've never seen it because he's always wearing a hat. If he does have hair, he probably doesn't like it because he's always covering it up.

Friday 18th Mar 2022

My form tutor spoke to me in form about last Friday because the evil receptionist emailed him. She told him I was being a knobhead or something and I told him she was the knobhead. Everyone overheard me. They all agreed though. She is.

We had to decide who sits on our tables at prom. I think we need a minimum of 8 people. We had a bit of trouble with the numbers. We included all the people in our friend group, but there still weren't enough. One of the people in our friend group is really fat, so I said he could take up 2 seats to solve the issue.

At break, Jack told me about a noise where if you listen to it, it makes you need to take a shit. He told me he listened to it and after about 30 minutes, he needed to take a shit. I think I might try it out for a laugh. He said I should play it while I sleep so that I shit the bed. I don't think that would be very funny for me at that point.

Speaking of shit, I saw a teacher walk out of the toilet. He had toilet paper stuck to his shoe. I didn't tell him, so I just watched him walk into his lesson with toilet paper on his foot.

Had a history exam today. It was my last exam. It went terrible. I accidentally wrote about the wrong extract, so I had to scribble out and rewrite an entire page.

I accidentally tripped over. I don't know if anyone saw. I tried to do that thing where you start skipping to try and make it look natural. I have no idea if it actually works or not.

I saw two butterflies dancing about together. They weren't actually bits of plastic floating about this time, so that was nice. They looked pretty.

When I got home, I noticed there are a bunch of ladybirds in my house. I don't know if they have a time of year where they come out or not. Anyway, they were everywhere. I keep having to put them outside. I think I might get fed up letting them outside soon because there are so many and they probably keep coming back. I think I'll just let the rest get stuck in my carpet and get eaten by my dogs or something.

It's Edward's party tomorrow. We're going bowling. I'm quite excited.

Saturday 19th Mar 2022

Had a beer with my brother and talked about girls and stuff. It was nice. I asked him if sex is all it's hyped up to be. He said it is, but it all depends on who it's with. You need to do it with the right person. He said if you can't have a laugh with them, they're not right because you need to be comfortable with them. I asked him about asking girls out. He said it should be more of a decision than a feeling. Romance isn't something you look for, but something you find. I'll remember that.

Went to the bowling party today. While driving there, I saw a crackhead riding a stolen bike. I could tell it was stolen because it was way too big for him. I don't need to explain how I knew he was a crackhead, they're pretty obvious to notice.

When I got to the party, I was 20 minutes early. I decided to wait outside. While waiting, a woman came up to me and asked if I had a spare lighter. I said I didn't. She then walked away and over to her group of friends. They also all looked like crackheads. Maybe they all just love hanging out at bowling alleys.

Eventually everyone turned up. Everyone except Edward. How can you turn up late to your own party? Knowing

Edward, I don't know why I was surprised. Seems like an Edward thing to do. Finally, he arrived.

I was worried we had to put bowling shoes on. I hate bowling shoes, they're very uncomfortable. Thankfully we didn't have to.

The bowling place smelled like cigarettes.

Edward was saying he wanted to have the bumpers up. We all made fun of him and said real men play with the bumpers down.

Turns out I'm shit at bowling. I haven't hit a single one yet. We all made fun of Edward for wanting the bumpers up, but I think I might need them.

My fat friend came to the party as well. When he bent down to roll the ball, I noticed he had a split in his trousers. I thought it'd be funny if we didn't tell him, but Jack told him anyway.

I came last in the end believe it or not. Nearly all of mine went in the gutters. The 6-year-olds in the lane next to us got a higher score than me. They got a score of 38 and I got a score of 32. In my defence though, they were playing with the bumpers up.

We went to the arcade afterwards. I thought I saw a lesbian couple. Turned out it was just a bloke with really long hair. I didn't see his beard until he turned around.

All the prizes in the arcade were absolute shit. Can you guess what the top prize for most tickets was? A fucking hairdryer.

What kid wants that? Imagine grinding to 8000 tickets and winning a hairdryer. I guess it's that or a bunch of shitty keyrings.

Monday 21st Mar 2022

Thought I saw roadkill at the bus stop this morning. Turned out it was just my hair getting in my eyes. Maybe it isn't a good thing I'm getting my own hair mixed up with dead animals.

We had an assembly. It was about self-portraits and how we see ourselves and how others see us. I thought it was going to be an inspirational talk about how to be the best version of ourselves. Turns out they just used it to complain about how some people weren't wearing the correct uniform. Of course they made it about that, I wouldn't expect any less from a school assembly. I remember one time they managed to link the Ed Sheeran song "Shape of You" to the Bible or something. How do you manage that?

Joseph told me about how he accidentally poured orange juice into his cereal instead of milk this morning because of how tired he was. We've all been there. I remember when I once did something similar. I was a good boy at school this one time and my mum gave me a KitKat. I got a bit mixed up and put the chocolate in the bin and ate the wrapper instead. I was very sad about that.

Edward has stopped bringing in stuff from his bin from home to show us and for me to write about because his mum keeps wondering how the bin keeps getting magically emptied without anyone touching it. This means my diary entries will probably be shorter from here on.

Some girl sprayed perfume in science. I felt like I was having an asthma attack. I don't even have asthma. I probably will do now.

Alvin was sucking on a lollipop. He turned around and called me gay. Have you seen how he was sucking it? He looks way more gay than me. He was sucking it like it was something else.

Tuesday 22nd Mar 2022

Read an article that about how paranormal experts are saying *"We are running out of ghosts"* because the old ones are dying off. That explains why you never seen a dinosaur ghost. They say it's to do with Wi-Fi or something. I honestly have no idea how a ghost can die, they're already dead.

I found some ripped out pages from a porn magazine while walking to the bus stop. There was literally just a bunch of pictures of naked women laying about in a bush on the side of the road. You bet I took a few of them. My lucky day!

Got my English exam back that I did last week. I had to write an article on sweatshops. I did a very good job talking about how they are bad. I got a grade 6. The guy sitting next to me wrote about how he likes sweatshops and how child labour is cost-effective. I guess it just goes to show that in your English GCSE, it doesn't matter what you write, it's how you write it.

Mark installed a virus on his laptop today at lunch. We all laughed at him.

I thought I'd try and impress the girls by doing press-ups. My mates pulled a funny joke on me by wiping bird poo on my back. If it's not a bird shitting on me, my mates will do it for them. Good to know. I look like a right twat now and I didn't impress anyone. Brilliant.

Wednesday 23rd Mar 2022

It's actually a warm and sunny day today. That's a miracle considering I'm in England.

Had PE. It was fucking boiling. My friend fell over and hurt her hand, so she asked the teacher for a plaster. The plaster she was given had a picture of The Muppets on it. If my plaster had a picture of The Muppets on it, I'd start feeling better instantly. I love The Muppets.

My mate told me a story in art about how someone climbed through his cat flap. He got really scared because apparently a paedophile had recently escaped from prison or something. Turned out it was just his neighbor's dog that came through the cat flap and not some nonce. He told me he had to break into his neighbor's house to return their dog. Don't know if I believe that bit.

Saw a butterfly at lunch. Edward asked me what came first between the butterfly and butter because he was curious what got named first. I said *"I don't know"* in a way that suggested to him that I didn't really care.

Because it's a nice and sunny day, I decided to lay in the sun. I was enjoying it until I got a ball kicked at my head. I can't enjoy anything.

My maths teacher is pregnant. She recently found out the gender of her baby. One of the girls baked a gender reveal cake. It was a girl. We all cheered and congratulated her. If I'm going to be honest with you, I didn't really care what gender her baby was, but the cake was nice.

In science, Noah told me a story about how he went on holiday to Greece and when he got back, his dog was ash. His grandad had cremated it without them knowing. Apparently, it had a heart attack or something. Noah has absolutely shit luck with animals. He told me about the time he watched his cat get hit by a truck. That's not a surprise though, most cats get hit by a truck.

Thursday 24th Mar 2022

There is a guy with really big ears that gets on my bus. They are genuinely huge. They say a big nose means a big penis, is there a similar thing for ears?

One of the people in my form said they think the Earth is flat. His argument was that aeroplanes fly in a straight line and not slightly tilted down so that they keep the same elevation above the Earth. He said if the Earth was round and you flew in a straight line, you'd fly off the Earth. He said he once brought one of those spirit levels onto a plane and that the bubble was in the middle, so the Earth must be flat. I couldn't be bothered to explain gravity to him because you just can't win an argument against a stupid person. They never listen.

Some knobhead was twanging a ruler in maths. It really started to piss me off. I eventually told him to shut up.

Literally nothing else happened at school. I think my days are getting more and more dull.

When I got home, I baked some cookies. I ended up eating more cookie dough that actual baked cookies. I think I might get salmonella. It tasted nice though.

I found an old diary of mine from 2017. That was like 5 years ago. I had a read. The first entry was me talking about some new waterproof camera I got. I tried it out on holiday. It got water inside it and broke. Typical. I don't think I've been more disappointed since. My writing hasn't changed much in the past 5 years.

I wrote about the time I went on holiday to America as well. I wrote that we visited a disgusting lake that smelled like shit. I remember that. It genuinely ranked of egg. America was weird. I remember seeing a flag that said *"God, guns and guts. America, let's keep all 3!"* I think that perfectly sums up America.

If you haven't guessed, I've got so few ideas I'm literally writing about my old diary. I'm writing a diary entry about a diary entry. I have stooped that low. That reminds me, I haven't written a poem this week. To be fair though, I did write 2 last week.

Friday 25th Mar 2022
I'm not the smartest man on Earth. I forgot to bring my diary into school today, so I'm writing this on a piece of scrap paper.

The bus journey was shit. There was a girl making weird and annoying noises. She sounded like if a cat got hit by a car. She might have been singing, but I couldn't tell because I had put my headphones on to drown it out.

A kid ran into me in the corridor. He then shouted at me saying I pushed him even though he ran into me. His other friends came over and started having a go at me. They were all year 7s. I don't think I want kids when I'm older.

In form, Rob got a really shitty song stuck in my head. It was the song Starships. I hate that song. I can never remember any of the lyrics either, so I just have *"Starships were meant to fly"* on loop in my head. Annoying.

We had a quiz in form. It's a quiz that the teachers make that is given to every form in the year. They put the questions on the electronic whiteboard, and we have to answer them. I was in one of the questions. The question was *"Who comes first in the register?"* I come first because my name starts with an A. When they showed the answers, they had a picture of me. It wasn't the most flattering picture of me because it's the picture they have on the register. I still look pretty good though.

We had PSHE, it was about drugs. We watched a video about them. The video was supposed to make us scared of drugs, but it actually made them look really fun. If anything, I want to try drugs after that video. Not a very good video then.

We were told about an EastEnders actress who snorted so much cocaine her septum fell out. Your septum is the thing that separates your nostrils by the way. This meant she just had one big nostril. That must have looked hilarious. Apparently, she had surgery to have a new one put in or something. I wonder if she can take it out and put it back in again like a glass eye. That'd be a cool party trick. Giving yourself one big nostril. Dunno if that'd make kids laugh or cry, it would be kinda weird.

I remember when I was younger, I saw a video of a man with no eyes playing piano. It scared the shit out of me. I thought he was a monster until I learned that people like that actually exist and that he was actually just disabled. I feel kinda bad for thinking that now.

Monday 28th Mar 2022

There was dog poo at the bus stop this morning. It stank. The worst bit was the bus was late, so I had to stand around and smell it for about 15 minutes.

I got into school late, so I had to go straight to assembly. Everyone was already sat down when I walked in. luckily there were a bunch of empty seats on the edge of the aisle. There was a pretty girl sitting on the edge next to an empty seat. I didn't go sit next to her though because I was a massive pussy. Wasn't that much of a loss though because you're not allowed to talk to people in assembly anyway. If I see her at prom, she might be on my list of people I want to dance with.

Got PE now. I didn't bring my PE kit in today because I hate PE. When the teacher came up to me to ask why I wasn't in kit, she got hit in the head with a basketball. That is exactly the reason I hate PE. Shit like that happens all the time.

While standing around waiting for PE to end I decided to talk to my mate who works on a farm. He kept sneezing because he has hay fever. I said it's probably not a good idea to work on a farm if you have hay fever.

Had maths next. My mate showed me some carpet burn on his arm. I asked how it happened and he told me he fell down the stairs and his arm rubbed on the carpet. I thought that story was kinda funny.

I keep finding shards of glass in my maths book. I think I might have accidentally smashed a glass or something while doing maths homework and didn't clean it all up. Some of it might have made its way into my bag. Can't be bothered to check though.

It's Gen's birthday today. We all had to sing happy birthday to her. I didn't want to because I don't like her. She's really annoying. She's the type of person who is always complaining about her anxiety and any minor inconvenience. She needs to shut up sometimes.

Saw a really hot girl at lunch. I wish I'd brought my sunglasses in today. You know how people can't see what you're looking at when you wear sunglasses? Exactly! You can look at all the hot girls without them knowing. Genius.

Talked to that flat Earth kid again. He says France doesn't exist. He said he has been to France, and it looks suspiciously similar to Belgium. He now thinks France doesn't exist and when you go to France, you actually go to Belgium.

Edward had brought in an Obi-Wan Kenobi action figure. We thought it would be funny to crucify him on a fence. We said Edward should bring in his other toys so we can re-enact the last supper. It is nearly Easter time after all. By the end of the year, we would have acted out the whole Bible with Star Wars toys.

Tuesday 29th Mar 2022

There was a moth on the bus this morning. One of the annoying kids had crushed it and was throwing it at people. After he had finished having his fun and being a knobhead, he didn't really know what to do with it. He said to pass it to some fat girl because she'd eat it. She'd eat anything he said.

In English, we've been practicing our creative writing skills for out GCSE. They have been giving us pictures and we have to write a story about them. We were given a picture of an old man looking in a mirror, and in the mirror was a younger, more handsome version of himself. I wrote that he had some sort of new illness that was like the opposite of anorexia where he sees himself as being more attractive than he actually is. I'm pretty good at creative writing.

Got into an argument with that flat Earth kid again. He says he needs to see it to believe it. I said we have seen it and we literally have photos of it. He says he needs to see it in person because he thinks it's edited footage. I got fed up with him and said, *"Well you've never seen wet pussy, doesn't mean it's not real!"* He said he has seen it in porn. I mocked him by saying it might be edited footage. I can't believe how much I absolutely shat on him.

Edward brought in a top hat. It was one of those magician's hats with a compartment in the top to put a rabbit in or something. I tried it on. I looked like Willy Wonka because of my curly hair. When Edward put it on, he looked more like the Monopoly man minus the moustache.

I quite like this hat. It'll help prevent more birds from shitting on me. I need to buy a hat. I'd quite like a fedora. I've always been a fedora type of guy.

I think Edward has started bringing his rubbish in again. What a relief. I was starting to get really bored. He did say that the charity shop where he gets most of his rubbish from is shutting down though. That'll suck. At least he'll still have his bin from home to get his stuff from.

Wednesday 30th Mar 2022

Talked to my brother about wanting a fedora. He told me not to get one because he said a fedora is a paedophile hat. He says the only people that wear them are nonces. A bit awkward then because I think it would suit me.

My PE teacher encouraged me to do some revision during PE because I never participate. I asked them if I'm allowed my phone to do some science quizzes because that's the only sort of revision I'm good at. They said I'm not allowed on my phone because of school rules. Don't see why I'm not allowed my phone if I'm only using it for revision. Stupid rule. Guess I'll just watch everyone else play basketball instead.

A girl came up to me and asked me if I could tell her a story because she was bored and I'm always telling people stories. I told her about the time I went to a bowling alley that was filled with crackheads. She loved it. She then stood up and leaned in front of me to watch the people play basketball. I was trying really hard not to stare at her arse.

Talked to my fat friend. I asked him about how he jumps in swimming pools. I asked him if it's possible for him to do a pencil jump, or can he only do a cannonball?

Art was weird. We had to work on our texture project. I chose to do a cityscape painting using thick black lines. The girl opposite me completely copied my idea. She literally did exactly the same thing I did. That's not the annoying bit. The annoying thing was she did it better than me.

I tried using a palette knife to scrape the paint on for the buildings. I couldn't find one, so I ended up scraping the paint on with the edge of my ruler instead. My ruler ended up covered in black acrylic paint. It looked like I'd shoved it up my arse. That's the same ruler I use for everything, so I might get some weird looks.

I tried experimenting with adding some white highlights, but the paint was still wet, so it just ended up smearing everywhere. It looked like a giant bird shat on my buildings. I'm rubbish at art.

Thursday 31st Mar 2022

Read an article about a thousand-year-old mummy that was wearing Adidas trainers. Apparently, they found it somewhere in the mountains and it probably died of a head injury. I have no idea how it had those trainers on, because Adidas wasn't around 1000 years ago. Maybe she was just really good at making shoes and they just happened to be as good as modern-day Adidas. Your guess is as good as mine though.

Thought I'd write a poem about that mummy wearing Adidas trainers.

"Mummy in the mountains, she was wearing Adidas shoes.
Adidas weren't around back then, might be fake news.
They say she died of a head injury, so a helmet would have been a better decision.
Trainers aren't gonna help you if you if your head and a big rock have a collision.
Living in the mountains, Adidas isn't what I'd take.
She clearly thought otherwise, what a silly mistake.
Mummy in the mountains, she's a thousand years old.
Adidas weren't around back then, how did she get them if they weren't being sold?"

We had a room change in skills. We were moved to an art room. There was a large painting of a naked woman. It had it all. Everything except arms and legs because it was that type of art. Like in ancient Greece or something where none of the statues had arms or legs. Anyway, it showed all the interesting bits if you know what I mean. I took a photo of it.

It started snowing. I don't think it will snow enough for anything interesting to happen though. It'll probably only snow for about 5 minutes knowing England.

I had finished my skills work, so they gave me an Easter egg to colour in because it's easter soon and the art department wanted a bunch of coloured eggs for something. When I had finished colouring it in, it looked like a Jimi Hendrix album cover. Very colourful and reminds you of LSD.

I would be looking forward to Easter, but I'm just gonna be worrying about revision the whole time because I've got my GCSEs soon after.

I was wrong. It's still snowing. The thing is though, it won't settle because the ground is too wet. That just means the snow melts and turns to water as soon as it touches the floor. Might as well not be snowing then. All it means is that I'm freezing and I'm not even getting any proper snow. Rubbish.

We weren't allowed in the usual break area because the year 10s were having exams in there. This meant I had to stand around in the cold.

Gen had a bandage on her arm in maths. She was showing it off to everyone. I hate Gen, she's such an attention seeker. Apparently, she had a surgery to have an implant put in that means she can't get pregnant. Don't see the point in her getting that, I can't imagine anyone wanting to have sex with her.

Edward brought in a burrito at lunch. He started eating it from the side. The side! You don't eat a burrito from the side, you eat it from the top. He was eating it like a fucking watermelon. He got filling everywhere. What an absolute idiot!

Edward also brought in something he bought from a charity shop for us to piss around with. He brought in a Batman clock. It was just a normal clock, but with a picture of Batman on it. We had the great idea to take down one of the school clocks and replace it with the Batman one. It might annoy a few people because the Batman clock had no batteries, so it didn't do anything, but it looked great.

Friday 1st April 2022

I'm not going to continue this diary anymore. No more poems, no nothing. I can't be bothered.

Just kidding, April Fools' Day bitch!

I was planning on pranking Edward by telling him it was home clothes day, so he would be the only one to come in wearing home clothes. Never got round to it though.

In form, we did a quiz. We do a quiz every Friday. I was in last week's quiz remember? I assumed that all of the questions were going to be trick questions because it's April Fool's Day. The first question was *"What's the largest lake in Africa?"* I put that it was a trick question because Africa doesn't have any lakes because there's no water there. Turns out I was wrong, and they actually do.

We were given a voting thing where you vote who gets the award for funniest person in the year, or best couple, or biggest chatterbox or something. I hope I get voted as funniest person. I tried voting myself for that one to try and increase my bets. Everyone else probably tried the same thing for that one though. Everyone thinks they're way funnier than they actually are. Michael is a good example. He thinks he's hilarious, but he's actually just a knobhead.

At break, I saw a kid on his phone. He was on YouTube. I caught a glimpse of his recommended. I saw a video titled *"Condom taste tier list"*. I wish I never looked.

In science, there were these two guys high on drugs. They told me it was acid or something. They were being pricks and stealing my stuff and throwing it about. I got sick of them and called them knobheads. The teacher overheard me and sent me outside. She asked what's going on. I said those guys were high on drugs and they were pissing me off. The next lesson, they got taken out of our lesson by the deputy head. Their friend leaned into me and whispered that if they are in deep trouble because of what I told the teacher, I was going to get the shit kicked out of me. He called me a *"snitch"*. He said if I was lucky, I'd only get a broken nose. That doesn't sound too fun. It's not my fault they were doing drugs in school. Don't complain to me if your friends are retards.

I was quite scared to be honest with you. That group of friends are quite violent. They're all drug addicts too. They were talking about doing cocaine recently. I guess those videos they show us in PSHE really don't do much.

I spent my entire lunchtime hiding from them so that I didn't get beaten up.

I wonder what will happen on Monday about all this then. Maybe they'll do more drugs and forget about it or something.

Monday 4th April 2022

There was a dead fly with a million eyes on my windowsill this morning. Normal flies have two big eyes, but this one just had a head made of them. Our house is nearly 400 years old, so God knows how long that's been there. It might be an ancient species of fly that died out hundreds of years ago. You never know.

We had an assembly. They read us a Dalai Lama quote. It was something like *"Be kind whenever possible. It is always possible."* I hope those drug addicts were listening to that. I'm not exactly in the mood to get beaten up today. If you didn't know, the Dalai Lama is some sort of an important bloke in Buddhism. He's sort of like the Buddhist version of the Pope, but not really. That's just an interesting fact to throw at you. Who says you don't learn anything talking to me?

Had PE first. The whole year does PE, so if I were to get beaten up, now would be the time. To my surprise though, none of them did anything. I mean yeah, I got a few looks, but nothing else aside from that. Maybe that Dalai Lama quote did something.

I was really expecting to get the shit kicked out of me. It's not like they haven't done it before. I remember once a while back, I slapped one of them in science because they were being stupid and flicking hydrochloric acid about. I tried to stop them by grabbing their hand and they slapped me, so I slapped them back. Their friends found out and weren't too happy, so at lunch they dragged me behind science. I felt like I was going to be publicly executed. They then took it in turns slapping the shit out of me. All because I tried to prevent corrosive acid going in someone's face. Anyway, that was a while ago, so maybe they've changed since then.

If they are going to beat me up, they have a week to do it because we have the Easter holidays next week. I'm going on holiday to somewhere in Scotland during Easter. That's probably the worst place to go on holiday. It's freezing there. I told my mum I would get very bored, but she said I can go walk wherever I want. I said I would be scared of being kidnapped. She said she joined a Facebook group chat with the locals, and she says they are all lovely. She was probably only talking to the elderly in the community then because I've never met anyone under the age of 40 who uses Facebook. I've also never met an old paedophile, so that didn't do much to comfort me. If you're old, you'd be a shit kidnapper. All the nonces aren't on Facebook, so there's no way she could know if all the people are friendly. All the nonces are on Instagram. If she started a group chat on there, I'd be much happier.

We got our mock exam results in maths. You need 70% to pass! That's a load of bollocks. I only got 56%. I don't need maths to get into the college I want, so I might slightly give up on maths and focus more on the other subjects because 70% is a scam.

I asked Mark if there are any hot girls in Scotland because he's Scottish. He's also the bloke who keeps sneezing in my hair. He said most of the girls in Scotland are ginger, so I should be prepared for disappointment. Although, in my old school I had a Scottish RS teacher who was fit. She was also brunette and not ginger, so you never know.

In science, Noah told me a story about how he nearly killed his cat with a Nerf gun. He said he was acting like James Bond and accidentally shot it.

We had a cover teacher in science. She was really fat. She had all chin and no neck. Don't call me mean for saying that by the way, she was a nasty person. She deserves it.

Tuesday 5th April 2022

I saw a man doing DIY in his garden while on the bus this morning. He was building a brick wall. I could tell it was DIY and that he wasn't a professional brick layer because he was doing a really shit job. He wasn't smoothing out the cement as it squeezed out the sides as he pressed the brick down. I'm not a professional brick layer myself, but I know that's not how you lay bricks. You need to scrape the excess cement off the sides otherwise you just get clumps of cement sticking out everywhere. It really pissed me off. Not only that, but the entire wall was wonky. I could probably do a better job.

I was looking out of the bus window on the other side of the bus because the sun was in my eyes if I looked out of the window on my side. The girl sitting next to that window keeps staring at me though. She's giving me some sort of evil glare. I think it's because the thinks *I'm* the one staring at her because I'm looking out of the window next to her. It felt like a very awkward staring contest I wasn't competing in. I think I won though because she was looking at me which meant the sun was in her eyes. The whole reason I was looking over to her was because I was getting sun in my eyes, but now I've sort of passed that issue on to her. I guess we both just got very annoyed at each other.

The desks in English are always messed up. The English department have all their meetings in our English room, so they leave the tables in a weird way. I tried getting to my table, but Chris (the fat kid) was in the way. Thought I'd write a poem about him.

"Fat, greasy, smells like fudge; Chris is so heavy, he wouldn't budge."

It's quite a grey day today. It was sunny on the bus, but it was pretty grey and gloomy from then on. I thought I heard thunder in one of my lessons, but it turned out it was just a bloke pushing a wheelie bin.

At lunch, we stood around outside PE and watched the girls play netball. Don't ask. Anyway, Edward pointed out that Cambridge University Netball Team have a really unfortunate name. CUNT. He's got a point.

We started making jokes about what Edward would be like on drugs. Jack then told us a story about the time he went on an RS trip, and they stopped off at a petrol station. There was a dispenser in the toilets. You could put £1 in and get some mints. He said the mints tasted like shit. He handed them to his mate and told him to have a taste. It was only then that they decided to read the wrapper and realised that they weren't mints, they were Viagra. He was wondering why they were selling food in the toilets. That is a weird place to have a sweet dispenser. That's a hell of a mistake to make on an RS trip.

Pushed on a pull door again. I sometimes think it would be handy to be Darth Vader so that you could use the force to check if it was a push or a pull door. It would save me a lot of embarrassment.

Wednesday 6th April 2022

The bin men don't come on Wednesdays, but I noticed a bunch of bins laying about on the path while walking to the bus stop this morning. Usually if there's bins knocked over, it means the bin men left them like that. Maybe they've just been left like that since yesterday. Either way, it annoyed me because I had to walk on the road to get around them.

My mate had an operation on his ankle recently because he plays a lot of rugby, and these things happen. He let me mess about on his crutches. I never realised how much balance is needed to work those things. The number of times I fell into a wall was crazy.

He had his foot in a cast. He was complaining about how much his feet stank because he couldn't wash them because of the cast. Me and my mates had the genius idea to spray deodorant in his cast to fix the smell he was complaining about. He ended up complaining even more because it made his feet cold and sticky. No one's ever satisfied with anything.

I held the door open for everyone while walking to PE. I didn't get a single thank you. Ridiculous!

I haven't been shat on by a bird in ages. I just noticed that. I think it's because I've been choosing to stay under shelter whenever possible. I remember I nearly got shat on while waiting for the bus a few days ago, but it just barely missed me. I'll try to keep that up.

I got science now. I walked in and sat down. I looked around and thought *"Hang on a minute… I don't know any of these people…"* Turned out I had walked in the wrong class. I was let out early from PE, so I walked in on some year 9's lesson. I was too embarrassed to get up and walk out because that would have attracted more attention to me, so I just sat there and waited for their lesson to end and mine to start. I'm a fucking idiot.

When my actual lesson started, we got given our physics mock papers back. I actually did insanely well. I got 82%. I think I did the best in my whole class. Maybe I'm not completely retarded after all.

Thursday 7th April 2022

Read an article about a UFO expert who admitted that his many years of UFO spotting might have been a result of his dodgy eyesight. This is one of the few articles I've read that have actually made sense. The funny thing is that I then found another article shortly after about a professional spoon bender who claims he got his powers when he was young because of an encounter he had with a UFO. Judging by the fact he's a professional spoon bender, I wouldn't take his word for it. I just thought it was funny that the first bloke genuinely believed he was seeing UFOs but then realised they were because of his shit vision, whereas the second bloke is completely bullshitting because spoon bending is a party trick, not alien technology.

We had homework due today. Rob said he forgot it because he was going to do it last night, but he didn't get round to it because *"Shit literally hit the fan."* That's a weird homework excuse. That's like taking the dog ate my homework to another level. Having someone shit on a fan is pretty weird.

Never mind, he just explained to me it's a phrase and he didn't actually mean it literally, even though he literally said, "*shit **literally** hit the fan*." I don't think people should say the word "*literally*" if it's a phrase. I think it ruins the point of it being a saying, you know what I mean? Don't blame me for thinking someone literally shat on a fan which resulted in him not doing his homework. He did say the word "*literally*" alright. I'm not stupid for that.

Apparently, we have leavers' day on the same day as prom night. That is completely retarded because that's not even our last day. You can dress up as whatever you want on leavers' day. My mates and I were talking about what we wanted to come as. I think I'll come in dressed as Spider-Man.

I'm planning on playing the greatest prank ever on leavers' day. My plan is to fill an inflatable sex doll with helium and letting it go in the sports hall. I chose the sports hall because it has the highest ceilings, so they wouldn't be able to get it down. I have no idea how I would fill it up though. Helium canisters are quite expensive, and I can't exactly take it down to the card shop and go "*Hi, could you fill this up for me please?*" I'll figure it out later.

When I got home, there was some bloke going door to door selling stuff. My dad says they're dodgy people because they might have a look inside your house through the front door when you open it to see if there's anything they want to nick. Apparently, they like stealing things. My dad opened the door. The man said *"Hi, sorry to disturb you but..."* *"Sorry, I'm not interested"* my dad said as he shut the door in his face. Fair enough. To be honest though, there's not many valuables to steal in our hallway, so he didn't miss out on much. Unless he likes family photos.

Friday 8th April 2022

I ran out of shampoo this morning, so I had to use bodywash instead. I see nothing wrong with that. I'm pretty sure every bloke in the world has done that at some point.

It's the last day of term until the Easter holidays. That doesn't really mean anything to me though because I'm just going to be doing revision for most of the holidays, so it's not much of a break. I'm going to Scotland for the second week of the holidays, but I doubt that'll be any good because it's Scotland. I mean yeah, it looks nice, but that all goes out the window when your balls have shrivelled inside you from the cold. You're no longer thinking *"Oh, what a lovely view"*, you're thinking *"Fuck me it's freezing, I want to go home."*

We did an Easter quiz in form. One of the questions was *"How many times could the amount of jellybeans Americans eat at Easter wrap round the Earth?"* The answer was 2 times. That's a complete lie. I reckon one American eats enough jellybeans to wrap round the world at least once.

While walking to history, I got into one of those awkward situations where someone is walking towards you, and they try to get past. They step to one side to get around you, but you do the same thing to get around them. This results in you both continuously stepping in front of each other. Do you know what I mean? Anyway, I tried doing that thing cyclists do when they indicate where they are going to turn on a road. It worked. I am a genius.

I fell in a hole while walking to science. The ground was really uneven, and the grass was really long, so I couldn't tell. I looked like a right twat.

The girls on my table in art were showing me the prom dresses they ordered. I couldn't care less.

I saw a sixth former wearing a blue top and no bra. I could tell she wasn't wearing a bra because you could see her... you know. That's probably the most interesting and exciting thing I've seen all week.

I just saw an autistic kid eating his own earwax. I take back what I said earlier, this is probably the most interesting thing I've seen all week.

When I got home, a bloke was there to pick up something we sold him on eBay. He stank of onion.

Sunday 10th April 2022

We had an extension on the house a few years back. That extension is now my brother's bedroom. His new bedroom window overlooks my bathroom window. The bottom half of my bathroom window is frosted so that you can't see in, but the top half isn't because the people who designed the bathroom weren't expecting people to be able to look in from above. This means my brother can see me whenever I'm taking a shit. The worst bit is that the window that overlooks my bathroom is the same window that his desk is facing, so he's always looking out of it. I'm always scared he and his girlfriend spend all their spare time watching me wipe my arse. I wouldn't put it past them.

I'm fucking knackered because I didn't get much sleep last night. I'm supposed to be doing revision, but I can't focus on it. I was up all night because my brain was doing that thing where it plays back all the old memories of embarrassing things you've done throughout your life. I kept thinking about the time a girl I kinda liked invited me to a party. It was a party involving alcohol, not a bowling party. I got a bit drunk and took my shirt off. I can't remember why, but I think it was to impress her. I then went home and realised I had left my shirt at her house. She then had to hand it to me the next day in a carrier bag. True story. I'm not very good with girls.

Saw a Spider-Man costume review on YouTube. It was some fat bloke dressed as Spider-Man. Spider-Man costumes are one of those things where it doesn't matter how expensive the costume is, if you don't have the right body type, you look like an utter idiot. If you're skinny and dressed as Spider-Man, you look great, but if you're fat and dressed as Spider-Man, you look nothing like him. You're just a fat bloke in spandex at that point. Makes sense though, Spider-Man gets lots of exercise.

My brother had to go save his mate by picking him up from his girlfriend's house because her mum walked in on them having sex. Apparently, she just walked in without knocking to give them sausage rolls. I don't know If I would want to have sex in my house while I'm living with my parents. Too risky.

I remember my brother had his girlfriend round this one time and they were both piss drunk. I was sitting in the living room and watching a movie with my mum and dad when my brother casually walked down the stairs and into the kitchen naked, got a glass of water, and went back upstairs. My mum said, "*Is he wearing socks?*" She didn't even comment on the fact he was naked, just that he was wearing socks. That's not the question I'd be asking. It was quite clear he was naked. I later asked him if they were having sex at the time, and he said yes. Did I need to ask that? Pretty obvious they were to be honest. What else do you get naked for?

Monday 11th April 2022

I came up with a TV show idea. They should send an autistic atheist to the most haunted places in the world and see what happens. So, me basically, I'd be sent to haunted places. It'd be pretty interesting though. I'd watch it if it came on Netflix. I don't know if I'd be shitting myself or not. I say I'm not scared of ghosts now, but that all goes out the window when you're there doesn't it. I'm not all that manly yet either; I still get scared by the Michael Jackson Thriller music video. I might have the balls to do it in a few years' time though.

I think the ghosts would be more scared of me than I am of them. It'd be a bit like with spiders, you know how they're more scared of us than we are of them. Or at least that's what my mum always told me. I think the ghosts would be extra scared of me because I have autism. I'm a special breed. I'd be more scared of an autistic spider because it'd probably be less predictable. Same thing with me.

I've been spending a lot of my free time watching psychic fail videos. You know those people who claim they can talk to the dead? Yeah, they're full of shit and it's hilarious. Especially when they get it VERY wrong. I absolutely hate psychics. I think it's evil to take advantage of grieving people for money, so it's amazing to see them get humiliated.

Tuesday 12ᵗʰ April 2022

My brother told me a science fact today. He said that when someone farts, that's their shit molecules going in your nose when you smell it. He then farted on me after he told me that. I made sure to keep my mouth closed.

I kinda want to dig up my dead hamsters to see what they look like. They died 5 years ago, so they'd probably be all bones now. I think it'd be pretty interesting. You know what I mean?

I'm finally getting a haircut tomorrow. I've been moaning about that for ages. Everyone at school has been making fun of me for looking like an idiot, so that'll be problem solved. Actually, no it won't. Everyone always harasses you when you get a haircut and always comment on it. Every lesson you go to, you'll get people saying *"You got a haircut"* as though I didn't know. You don't need to tell me when I've had a haircut. I used to get people saying I look like Willy Wonka, I probably still will because it's gonna be a curly mess no matter what. I guess it'll just neaten it up a bit.

Thursday 14th April 2022

Going on holiday today. My brother unlocked the bathroom door with a penny while I was taking a shit this morning. I'm glad we're not taking him with us. He's staying at home with his girlfriend.

The car journey there is probably going to be longer than the actual holiday itself. We're stopping off at the Lake District first and staying there for the night. The trip to Scotland is too long to do all in one.

Thought I'd read some articles on the trip to cure my boredom. I read an article about some sea expert that is saying that the Loch Ness Monster might have been a whale's penis. He says that during mating sessions, sometimes the whale's dick will pop out of the water which may cause confusion among sailors. I imagine it would be disappointing for "*brave*" sailors to go out looking for a sea monster only for it to turn out it's just a whale's knob they're scared of.

My arse hurts like hell and I'm all achy. We stopped off at a KFC to get food. We ate it in the car though, so I didn't get to stretch my legs. I can feel the bones in my arse.

My dad asked me what I wanted from KFC. I said I wanted chicken. I don't know what he expected me to say. They don't really have much else on the menu.

I think there was some more news on the radio about what's going on in Ukraine. Couldn't hear it though because I was listening to Fireflies by Owl City on my headphones. I don't really like listening to all the horrible stuff happening on the news anyway.

During this million-year long journey, I've seen more animals than you would in a zoo. They were all dead in the road. I saw a video the other day about a professional roadkill chef. That's a quick and easy way to get every disease known to man. I would never eat at his restaurant. Sounds like the type of place you'd only find in China. They love mad foods like that, so maybe roadkill is some sort of delicacy.

We arrived at the hotel. It's a Georgian mansion. I said before that I don't believe in ghosts, but I think this place might change my mind. The haunted house ride at Disneyland looks less haunted than this place. The entrance was a big wooden door with stone statues on both sides. The whole place was built of dark oak and stone. What made the place feel extra haunted was the fact that they had a big moose head on the wall in reception. Whenever you see a haunted house in any movie, there's always a moose head on the wall. That's a fact.

I searched up the name of the hotel on google and the reviews were saying that they saw many ghostly apparitions. I wouldn't mind seeing a ghost because it would make a good diary entry.

I went for a stroll round the hotel to look for ghosts. I felt like Scooby-Doo. I saw they had a library, so I thought I'd start there first. It was hardly a library. It only had one bookcase and one big chair. Only a haunted house would have such a shitty design.

Thought I'd look upstairs. There was a big grand staircase. There were large oil paintings of old posh people on the walls. I guess they didn't have much to decorate with in Georgian times because every room is basically copy and pasted with the same sort of statues and paintings. I got bored and headed back to the hotel room.

Probably the scariest part of the haunted mansion is the fact it doesn't have Wi-Fi. Our room window overlooks some train tracks though, so I'll just watch trains go by instead. I have no complaints really because I have autism. A fun fact about autism is that every single one of us either love fire engines, trains, or dinosaurs. Speaking of dinosaurs, I've said before about how those ghost experts said old ghosts are dying off form old age and that's why you never see dinosaur ghosts. Maybe that's why I haven't seen any ghosts yet because Georgian times was a while ago. They also said they are dying because of Wi-Fi, so maybe not because there is no Wi-Fi here.

If I do get eaten by a demon tonight, I'm gonna be pissed off. I'm the last person you want haunting a place. An autistic ghost. Most ghosts would scare you; I'd probably just piss you off. I'd be the ghost that unplugs your phone in the night or something. Even worse would be a Tourette's ghost, I guess. That'd piss you off.

Friday 15th April 2022

I didn't end up getting eaten by a demon in the end. I told you ghosts aren't real. Although, I did wake up in the middle of the night to see a transparent young boy sitting at the foot of my bed and playing a game of cards. I definitely think it was my imagination though because I have no idea how to play cards and he was playing them exactly how I would. He was playing them very wrong. You don't need to know how to play cards to notice when someone's doing it wrong. If it was a real ghost, it was just as stupid as me.

We're back on the road again today. We're gonna be driving for another 7 hours. Yesterday was only a 4-hour drive and it was pissing me off. People say they live for the road and all that. They say they love it. They've clearly never been on a trip to Scotland. It makes your arse ache like mad from sitting down for too long.

After driving for about 2 hours, we stopped off at a restaurant for food. The restaurant was proper fancy. I could tell because it had fake bushes outside. Only posh places have fake plants. Especially bushes. Who has fake bushes?!

The inside was fancy as well. The walls were made of fake bricks. Like they had wallpaper of fake bricks. What's the point in that? You might as well just not plaster the walls or wallpaper them and get the same effect. Wallpaper bricks? Honestly, everything in this place is fake.

Can you guess what they had at the bar? I'll make it easy for you by saying it isn't real. It's wax fruit. Even the food is fake and it's a restaurant! Super fancy!

I imagine this place doesn't even sell real food and when you order food, they just bring you a LEGO set instead.

Turns out they did sell real food and it was actually quite nice. I had fish and chips. I then went to go use the bathroom. There was piss all over the floor. Maybe the restaurant wasn't all that fancy then.

"On the road again...do do doo do do... on the road again..." I dunno if I'm actually allowed to write the lyrics to that song or not because I don't know if I'll get fucked by copyright or something.

We finally entered Scotland. I could tell because of all the mountains and sheep. Did you know Scotland has more sheep than people? Interesting fact.

Scotland strongly reminds me of Skyrim. Mainly because of all the mountains and trees. This is because about 98% of Skyrim's gameplay is walking around mountains because you can't climb in that game. It also just looks like the type of place Vikings would live.

I saw a dead wolf on the side of the road. A fully grown dead wolf. Is that the kind of roadkill they have over here in Scotland?! We get hedgehogs in England, and they get wolves? I think I might want to spend this holiday indoors if that's the case.

We arrived at the inn we are staying at for the night. We're taking the ferry tomorrow morning and then we'll arrive at the place finally. It'll only have taken us about 3 days.

Saturday 16th April 2022

I don't know if they have autism in the animal kingdom, but I'm certain my dog has it. He threw up in the inn room we were staying at for the night. We were all worried because he threw up in the room, obviously, but it was all alright because he ate it all up again before we got the chance to try and clean it. Throwing up is your body's way of getting rid of things, that idiot just ate all up again. There wasn't a speck left. Saved us the work of cleaning it up though I guess.

Got on the ferry. I felt sick. I felt very bored as well because we were on the ferry for an hour. I went to the little shop area they had to go see if they had any magazines. They did, but they were just for old people. Makes sense because I haven't really seen any young people in Scotland. Maybe it's just a country for old people. That's probably the reason my mum likes it here so much and I don't. Anyway, all the magazines were meant for old people. There was one about lighthouses. Who wants to read a magazine about that? Apparently, there are only about 200 lighthouse keepers left in the world, so the demographic for that magazine is quite small.

They were selling other things in the shop too. I saw they were selling a Twister mat. I think Twister is the worst game to sell on a ferry because you can't play it. The boat is rocking about all over the place. It's simply not playable. They probably should have been selling Monopoly instead or something.

We drove straight to the beach when we arrived because we aren't allowed in the holiday home place until half five. The beach was freezing and windy. There were blobs of white foam on the sand. I heard somewhere that if you see that on the beach, it's whale sperm. Probably explains why there was a lot of it then. Whales must produce loads of the stuff.

I don't usually like going to the beach because I get sand all in my shoes. That's probably the worst feeling if you're autistic. This time was no exception and it really pissed me off.

When we got back to the car, I thought *"Oh fuck, where's my headphones?!"* Turned out I was wearing them, and I didn't notice I had them on because I had accidentally turned the volume off.

The beach wasn't as good as I wanted it to be. The last time I visited a beach was when I went to Cornwall, and I found a dead washed up sheep carcass. That was interesting. Nothing interesting here though. Maybe I'll find something interesting later. Maybe I'll find a dead cow or something.

We went to a restaurant for food. Until now, I haven't seen anyone Scottish who isn't really old. There was a waitress that didn't look much older than me. I thought she looked alright. She was ginger though. Maybe Mark was right when he said that all the girls here are ginger. That's a shame because I only really like brunettes.

They had bagpipes playing in the restaurant. I forgot Scotland had bagpipes. I would have thought twice about coming if I remembered that. I hate bagpipes; they are the most annoying instrument aside from the violin and the clarinet. It gave me a headache.

I'm really tired because my little sister was screaming at me last night because she's a twat. I was so tired that I started blowing on my ice cream to try and cool it down. I bet I looked like a twat. I think everyone's done that at some point though. I've done it before when I woke up early to catch a flight and had to quickly grab some breakfast. I was so tired I tried blowing on my Weetabix to try and cool it down even though I poured cold milk on it form the fridge. Maybe other people haven't done that and I'm just a special breed of retard.

My dad stopped off at a petrol station. I had a browse of the magazines they had since they didn't have any good ones on the ferry. I found some good ones. I'll have a read of them later.

We finally made it to the holiday house. It's alright. They had a gift basket with a bottle of gin inside. I didn't know how high in concentration of alcohol gin was, so I poured myself a full glass. It was only then that I realised it was a mistake, but I already poured it and added some tonic water, so I had to drink it. Bad idea.

Sunday 17th April 2022

It's Easter today. I would be happy about that, but I'm in a bad mood because I've got a headache. Probably from all that gin I had last night. I knew it was a bad idea.

Thought I'd make myself a cup of tea. I poured the water in the cup and waited for it to brew. I waited about 10 minutes before I realised I forgot to put the tea bag in.

We did an Easter egg hunt around the house. My little sister found an old Skittle in one of the cupboards and thought it was a really well-hidden Easter egg. I had to tell her to bin it because if she ate it, she'd get ill. God knows how long that's been sat there.

There is a step in the holiday home that's in between the kitchen and the living room. They had put a caution sign that they had made from laminated paper on the floor next to the step. I think I am more likely to slip on a small bit of laminated paper than on a step. Do you know how slippery laminated paper is when on a smooth surface? Very is the answer. It's like a game of ice hockey.

It could be a Home Alone trap. Just put some laminated paper on the floor. That's like double danger as well because of where they put it. You slip on the paper and then fall down the step.

It's a miserable and rainy day today, so I just stayed inside and watched a documentary on Hitler's genitals. It said that he only had one bollock and deformed genitals. I already knew all that, but I just saw it on Netflix and thought why not.

Monday 18th April 2022

Got my hand stuck in a towel rack this morning. I was trying to hang a towel on it and my hand got stuck. The bad thing was that it's one of those heated towel racks, so it burned.

It's absolutely pissing it down today, so I don't think I'll get up to anything.

Thought I'd have a read through the magazines my dad bought me at the petrol station a few days ago. I read an article on Uncle Fatty the monkey. It was about a monkey named Uncle Fatty who ate himself to death. Experts say he's dead, but they never found his body because monkeys apparently isolate themselves when they are dying because they don't want you to see them when they're weak. I don't understand how they never found him because he should be the easiest to find. The president of the We Love Monkey Club said that one day he was just gone. He can't have gone that far though. Unless he rolled away like a wheel.

Tuesday 19th April 2022

We went for a drive today just to have a look around. I've seen a lot of wind turbines. Makes sense, Scotland is probably the best place to put them because it's windy as shit here. I tried going for a walk the other day when it was windy. Terrible idea. It was blowing tiny droplets of rain into my face at very high speed. It felt like bullets.

We drove into town. It basically looked like if Birmingham was by the sea. That's the best description I can give of the place. We went there to buy me a wetsuit so I can go in the sea.

On the way back, I saw a sheep with a really long neck. It looked like a giraffe with wool.

When we got back, I put my wetsuit on and went straight to the beach. There was only one issue: I'm shit scared of the water. My parents blame it on the fact I watched Jaws, but I disagree because the movie Jaws actually made me feel better about the water. They killed the shark in the end didn't they. My fear of the water is so bad that I struggle to close my eyes in the shower.

The water was fucking freezing. I decided I was fed up after about 10 minutes, so I went to go play about in the sand dunes near the cliff edge instead. While building sandcastles, I noticed a small bone on the slope at the bottom of the cliff. I thought I'd investigate because there are probably other

105

bones because I've never seen an animal with just one big bone. Guess what I found at the top of the slope. A sheep skull. I told you I'd find bones at the beach! The sheep must have fallen from the cliff and died. Dunno where the rest of the sheep was though. It was just a thigh bone and a skull. I thought they'd look good in my room on top of my Ouija board, so I put the skull in my sandcastle bucket and took it back to the house.

I think it would be funny to bring it into school to show those crystal healing girls and tell them it's a cursed object or something to scare them. It's got horns, so they'd probably think it's extra evil.

Wednesday 20th April 2022

It's a terrible idea to have a bedroom wall be just one big window and then have that window overlook a road. Long story short, I get more people looking in on me than me looking out at them. Especially when I'm getting changed. I had an old woman drive past and stare at my knob and bollocks.

My parents decided to drag me along to see a church this morning. It was proper old and was from like the 1500s or something. There was a staircase that went to the top. Do you remember what I said a while back about old places having low ceilings? Yeah, this place was no exception. Going up those stairs was a nightmare. I kept tripping on the uneven stairs and smacking my head on the shitty low ceiling. I definitely think people were shorter back then. They had some old tombs with those engravings of the dead people laying on top. You know? It sorta looks like when Han Solo was frozen in carbonite. Anyway, the sculptures of the people inside were shorter than the average person today, so maybe I'm right. It would make sense. People live longer in the modern day, so we have more time to grow.

I went to have a look round the church graveyard. They had some of those above ground graves that were like a little stone box. I tried looking through the cracks to see if I could see any bones. I couldn't. I was very disappointed about that. We then went home.

My parents went to the beach again, but I stayed at home because I wanted to get some revision done. When they got back, they told me there was a wild pony on the beach and that it came up to them to say hello. I kinda regret staying at home now.

Thursday 21st April 2022

Literally fuck all happened today. We were gonna go out on a bike ride or something, but that never happened because the bike rental place gave us the wrong sizes of bikes.

Friday 22nd April 2022

If it isn't old women staring at my cock and balls, it's window cleaners. That's right, a window cleaner was at the house this morning while I was getting changed. The bad thing was that unlike the old woman who just drove past, this man had to slowly make his way round every window in the house. This house is practically made of windows. There's at least one in every room, so I was fucked. I had to seek refuge in a bathroom because the window in that room is frosted. We're leaving this place tomorrow, so it'll be good to get away from being stared at while getting changed in the morning.

We didn't do much today. We went to the beach, and I found a really old tobacco tin. It was covered in sand and other bits of sea life. I couldn't tell how old it was because all the info on the tin was covered by rust.

We brought buckets and spades to the beach. I decided to dig a big hole because that's what everyone does when they go to the beach. I got it to being about 4 feet deep but had to stop digging because it started to fill with water. We had to go home when my little sister threw sand in my little brother's eyes. She is such a little shit.

Saturday 23rd April 2022

We're going home today. Well...we're starting the trip home today. You know how long it took last time.

We packed all our stuff and left for the ferry. The ferry journey was alright. I fell asleep for the majority of it. We then got on the road again afterwards.

I noticed someone had sprayed messages on road signs saying about how the Coronavirus was made up by the government. I imagine that guy to be the type of bloke to sit at home on his own and dressed entirely in tin foil and surrounded by crucifixes. You know they're not a smart person when they try to get their message across to people by graffitiing it on road signs in the mountains. That's probably the worst place to spray them because no one goes down that road. He really isn't smart.

We stopped off at a public bathroom. Public bathrooms are probably the scariest place on Earth. Not only because there was some old man crying in one of the stalls for some unknown reason, but that the stall I was in had no toilet paper.

We arrived at the hotel we'll be staying at for the night. It's the haunted place we stayed at before. I survived last time, so I should be alright. I also survived that bathroom, so maybe I can survive anything. Although, if this diary does end abruptly, you can get a good guess why. I don't really care about being killed by a ghost though because my arse hurts too much for me to care about anything and I'm absolutely shattered. I've been sitting down for about 14 hours today. Fucking ridiculous!

Sunday 24th April 2022

I didn't get eaten by a demon again. I had the Ghostbusters theme song playing the whole night on loop to try and scare them off, so that could be why.

We got up early and went for breakfast. I had some little pastries. There was an old posh lady sitting on the opposite side of the room staring at me. She sort of reminded me of my English teacher.

We got back on the road again. This journey will be much shorter than yesterday's because we're no longer in Scotland, so it's mainly motorways form here on. Scotland is mostly slow moving and bendy roads.

After about five hours of arse ache, we arrived home. Finally. I got school again tomorrow, so I need to pack my bag and all that.

We ordered my prom outfit. I ordered a black suit with a bow tie.

Monday 25th April 2022

Everyone was staring at me on the bus this morning. I thought they were staring at my fresh trim I got over Easter, but it turned out a bird had shat in my hair without me noticing. I only noticed when I saw it in the reflection in the bus window. It was only a little bit though, so I just wiped it off with my sleeve.

When I walked into form, my mates started talking about my haircut. I had it cut much shorter because before I looked like a circus clown. The topic quickly went from talking about how nice my new hair was to how you could see my sideburns more clearly now that my hair is shorter. They were saying how they look like pubes on someone's testicles. I will shave them when I get home.

In maths, my teacher complimented my hair and said I was *"Rocking the sideburns."* I told her that people were telling me they looked like pubes on testicles, and she said that's outrageous. I'm still gonna shave them though.

At break, Edward had brought in a plastic Dory toy. You know the retarded fish from Nemo? We tried smashing it against a brick wall to smash it open, but it wouldn't crack. 7 times we threw it, and nothing. Maybe this is why Dory can't remember shit because we're smashing her against a wall. After about 10 minutes of throwing it into a wall, it finally smashed. The body was split into two halves and the eyes fell out. They were hollow and were like half spheres. Like contact lenses, but you can't see out of them. I had the idea to put Dory's eyes on mine and wear them like contact lenses and walk about. They made me look like some type of serial killer. I did look weird. At least that's what my friends told me; I couldn't see anything.

My mate was being a bit racist in skills. He said that all Indian people either own a corner shop or some sort of tech business. He then pointed out that Currys PC World is named Currys. See what I mean? That's not even that funny. Okay, it was kinda funny, but still racist. I guess he was only joking. Or maybe not, I couldn't tell.

I had a dentist appointment after school. I absolutely hate going to the dentist, but I do like nicking all the free samples of toothpaste they have in the reception area. The dentist appointment wasn't all that bad in the end. It did take a while though because my mum decided to have an hour-long chat with the dentist. She literally told the dentist her entire life story. I'm not joking.

My prom suit arrived. I tried it on. I look proper snazzy. I look like if Willy Wonka dressed for a funeral. (It's a black suit.) The bow tie looks nice on me. I'm the type of bloke who you can slap any old bow tie on and will always look amazing. I hope Grace will be impressed.

I shaved my sideburns as well.

Tuesday 26th April 2022

I saw the bin men at the bus stop this morning. One of them was making race car noises as he chased after the bin lorry. He looked like he was living the dream.

While on the bus, I read an article about a gorilla that had an addiction to smartphones. I don't see much wrong with that. I'd rather watch a gorilla play mobile games than just sit about. He seemed to be having a good time too.

Nothing else really happened today to be honest. I got my GCSE art exam tomorrow, so I don't know how to feel about that. I think it should be easy enough.

Wednesday 27th April 2022

Got my GCSE art exam today. It's like 12 hours long, so it'll be stretched across two days. This means it'll take up all of today and all of tomorrow.

I painted a city scape. I abandoned my original idea of thick black lines of paint for the buildings and used driftwood I painted black instead. I think that fits the theme of texture better. They give us a theme you see, and you have to make an art piece around that theme. I wrote in my sketchbook that I got the driftwood from my holiday to Scotland. I didn't, I got them from eBay.

We have one of those exam invigilators watching over us. I couldn't help but notice that all the invigilators I've ever had look no younger than 60. Probably because at that age you have nothing better to do than sit in a room for hours and watching people sit an exam.

I had a look what Edward was painting because he's in my art class. He had large, printed copies of his passport photo on his desk. He said he was going to cut them up and sew them together to make them look like Frankenstein's monster.

112

That's actually not a bad idea. Even though he already looks a bit like Frankenstein because he's just weird looking.

I finished early because sticking wood on a canvas doesn't take long. I spent the next few hours of the day typing BOOBS into my calculator. You do that by typing 80085 if you didn't know.

At break, Edward told me he no longer wants to be a librarian when he's older and wants to be a homeless artist instead. He says he wants to be that because apparently they don't have to pay taxes. I said being homeless is a shit way to try and save money because they have no money to save. He probably still wants to be one though because knowing Edward, that just went in one ear and out the other.

I told Edward a story about how I had a maths teacher in my old school who got hit in the head with a tuba and could no longer teach us. When I found out, I made a joke saying she had a *"brain tuba"*. I got told off. Still thought it was pretty funny though. I also told him the story of how I didn't used to know how people got money when I was younger. I thought you had to buy it. yes, I thought you had to buy money. I asked my dad how much £5 was worth. He said £5. I had no idea where people got money from then. I then thought maybe cash machines gave you free money because my dad would put has card in, press a few buttons, and money would come out. That isn't the case either. I really was a stupid kid.

I accidentally punched myself in the face. I was trying to pick up my bag, but it wasn't as heavy as I thought, so I picked it up with too much force. That sent my hand flying towards my face. It hurt quite a lot.

Thursday 28th April 2022

My shoes for prom arrived. They look nothing like the picture. These have massive pointy toes. They look like elf shoes. The picture made them look normal.

Got my 2nd half of my GCSE art exam today. I've already finished, so I might just work on my sketchbook instead.

We had to wait like 15 minutes before the exam because people hadn't shown up yet. My mates thought it'd be a good idea to kick a football about in the pottery room. It wasn't. They then had the great idea to put the football on the potter's wheel and watch it fly off. Another bad idea: I'm sure you can imagine why.

The exam was going to start soon, so we all left the pottery room acting like nothing ever happened.

The exam invigilator we have today looks half dead. She looks fucking ancient. I reckon she saw the pyramids being built.

We were all sitting in silence. That was until the fat kid sneezed and it scared the shit out of everyone. Even the teacher jumped. He then pulled out a family size bag of crisps and started munching on them. I don't think it was a good idea for them to allow snacks in the art exam.

The teacher goes round handing out biscuits every now and then. I saw the fat kid take two.

The bloke sitting next to me keeps swearing at me. I dunno why; I've done nothing to him. I even cleaned out his water pot and gave him some of my own paints and he still seems moody. He's like that all the time though and he's probably stressed about the exam.

They have magazines in the art room. I think they have them so students can cut out bits for collages or something. They had a women's fashion magazine, so you already know I had a look through that one first. Indeed, there were *images.* I got bored with it after about 10 minutes though and I noticed they had a ghost magazine that looked way more interesting.

I tried passing notes to the guy sitting next to me to strike up a conversation. He just scrunched them up and put them in the water pot. I guess I won't try that again then.

Someone whipped out a hairdryer and started drying their work. Brilliant, now I have some fat kid munching on crisps and some idiot with a hairdryer.

I got some blue acrylic paint on my black school jumper. They say acrylic paint doesn't come out, so I had the genius idea to paint over the acrylic paint with more acrylic paint that blends in with my jumper. It looks good as new. Except that bit of my jumper just looks a bit shiny now.

One of my mates started chatting up the invigilator. Dunno what he was saying, but it looked like sparks were flying. I know he gets no girls, so I wouldn't put it past him. To be fair to him though, she might have looked good... in dinosaur times. I think he tried shooting his shot 65 million years too late.

Friday 29th April 2022

I ate an insect this morning. It flew into my face and fell into my face mask (I wear a face mask on the bus because of COVID). I thought it fell out, but when I got on the bus, I realised that wasn't the case. I didn't want to pluck it out my face mask because I didn't want people looking at me and thinking why I just pulled an insect out of my mask. That would be some sort of weird magic trick. Anyway, I didn't want people thinking I'm weird, so I ate it. It was bigger than I thought. It took about 5 chews to finish, and I could still feel it in my throat after.

In form, Rob told me he doesn't understand why people care so much about what others think about them. I said it's funny he said that because that's the reason I ate the insect.

I got scared by my own reflection. I was going to open one of those glass doors and I saw my reflection and thought I was going to walk into someone when I opened the door. It was just my reflection though.

I told my mates about swallowing the insect. I said I was worried because my stomach feels funny, and I saw a video the other day about a guy who died from eating a slug. They told me a story about a woman who also swallowed a fly, so she also swallowed a spider to kill the fly, a bird to kill the spider, a cat to kill the bird, a dog to kill the cat, and so on. I wonder if that woman was Chinese. They would eat all that stuff.

I came up with a really funny joke about my bank password, but I can't tell you it because it involves you knowing my bank password. What a shame.

I got a 3-day long weekend because it's a bank holiday Monday. That means I'll have nothing to write about on Monday either then.

I don't feel all that bad about the insect anymore, so that's good.

Tuesday 3rd May 2022

It's my brother's birthday today. He's turning 19. I got him a box of sweets and a card that says *"With age comes wisdom. And a saggy ballsack. Happy birthday!"* I'm sure he'll love it.

Read an article about a man whose penis fell off. Apparently, it just fell off when he was on the toilet. That would suck wouldn't it. It had to be attached to his arm before it could be put back on his crotch area because of lack of oxygen or something. He had to wait about 6 years for it to finally be put back on properly. You know how slow the NHS can be sometimes.

I haven't done a poem in ages. I can't remember the last time I did one. Might as well write a poem about the bloke whose penis fell off.

"Hubble bubble toilet trouble
Knobless and looking a mess; it would be a shock to see him
undress
His knob on his arm and nothing in his pants
The only way forward is knob transplants

117

Has to wear long sleeve shirts or else there will be an
awkward situation
We can't have it on his arm, let's put it back to its old location
6 year waiting list
I imagine whenever he goes for a piss, he gets knob juice
down his wrist"

Nothing really happened at school today. When I got home, the sex doll and helium canister arrived. Leavers' day is Friday, so I'm gonna need it for then. That's only 3 days away. By the way, I've decided against asking Grace to be my date to prom. I am going to ask her to dance with me instead. I wonder how that will go.

Wednesday 4th May 2022

Happy Star Wars Day! I personally don't really care that much about Star Wars. I once thought stormtroopers were from Star Trek.

I tried helping a man at the bus stop this morning. His bus arrived and he hadn't turned up yet. I saw him running round the corner, and I saw the bus start to pull away. I ran to the front of the bus and waved at the bus driver to get him to open the doors and told him a man was coming to get on. The bus driver said "*I know*" in a really nasty tone of voice for some reason. I never got a thank you from that other man either. That made me sort of angry.

I read another article on the bus. I'm trying to stay well read because I've got my English GCSE soon. I read an article about a tank of syrup that collapsed and caused a flood of more than 2 million gallons of syrup. Apparently 21 people died. I don't know how that happens. I could easily outrun golden syrup. Although, it was in America, so the people probably ran towards it. It happened like 100 years ago, so it's probably no longer a sensitive subject so I can talk about it.

When I got into form, my mates asked me if I've been smoking because apparently I smell like smoke. My brother burnt some popcorn last night and left the burnt popcorn in the kitchen. I spend a lot of my time in there, so that's probably why.

Had a bit of a predicament today. I have a mate, Oscar. (He's one of the blokes in my skills class.) I saw him and Grace laughing with each other at break. I thought they were just having a laugh, but one of my mates told me they've been getting really close lately and have been sitting next to each other on the bus and stuff, and apparently, he invited her to his house for *"revision"*. You know what that means. My mate told me they're apparently dating now. I felt an awful sting in my brain.

I feel miserable. I haven't felt like this in years. An almost overwhelming feeling of jealousy and some sort of betrayal. He was my mate, and he knew I liked her. I feel like my confidence has been crushed too. That completely fucks over all my plans for prom. My friends caught me crying a bit in art. I must have looked a right pussy.

I have Oscar in my maths class, so I asked him about it then. I asked him if they did anything together, and if they have anything going on. He said they are nothing like that and are just friends. He told me he's dating some other girl, so he can't possible be dating her. He showed me the pictures of the girl he was actually dating and said that I shouldn't worry. That's a relief. What a fuss about nothing.

Maybe my plans haven't been fucked then.

Thursday 5th May 2022

I've been planning to dance with Grace, but I've just realised something. I have no idea how to dance *with* someone. Thought I'd do some research into dances. The tango… the waltz… the macarena… yeah, I can't do any of these. I guess I'll just stick to practicing my moonwalk then.

In skills, Nancy (the girl who shows me her sex videos) got me to sign her shirt because it's leavers' day tomorrow and everyone will be in home clothes or dressed up, so we had to sign each other's shirts today. She made me sign her boobs. Of course she did.

Most of the people in my school are drug addicts, so they were asking each other to draw a spliff on their shirts. A spliff is the thing you use to smoke weed by the way. The drawings weren't any good because the people drawing them are retards. It didn't end up looking like a spliff at all. It looked more like a mint Cornetto.

I didn't want to get my shirt signed because it'll just sit in my wardrobe gathering dust. I'll never look at it again. Pointless. I also don't want people signing my shirt because they'll just draw a massive cock and bollocks or something. Someone had written "*I love kids*" on Alvin's back in big letters and he hadn't noticed. As if he didn't already look like a massive idiot.

One of my mates asked me to sign their shirt, so I just put an @ to my Instagram on his back. He's now a walking advertisement for me. Genius.

My mates were playing a game where you had to draw an x where you thought the other person's nipple was. It's like a weird version of pin the tail on the donkey. We then labelled the right nipple as being *"Rob's favourite"*.

My Indian mate has *"Sex is £12.50"* and *"BJ is £10"* written on his back. We wanted to write tikka masala on his back, but he said that was too far.

I'm dressing up as Spider-Man tomorrow. I have noticed a bunch of moths in my house recently. I hope they don't eat my Spider-Man costume. I don't see what they get from eating clothes. Surely, they can't taste all that good. Although, in my primary school, there was this girl that was always chewing on her sleeve, so maybe not then.

Friday 6th May 2022

Today is the day I pull the greatest prank ever. I am going to fill a sex doll with helium and let it go. But let's start from the beginning of the day.

I am spending the day dressed as Spider-Man. There is one very big complication though. The bulge. I had bought something called a dance belt which I think is what male ballerinas wear to cover their bulge. The thing is though, it's basically a thong. I am going to be spending the day in a thong and dressed as Spider-Man. Brilliant.

My dad drove me in today because I couldn't really get the bus dressed as Spider-Man. The lenses practically blind you, and I've fallen off the bus before when I wasn't blind. Also, it would look very strange. Rows of people dressed normally and just one Spider-Man sitting there. Also because I had to bring in the sex doll and a small canister of helium and that would be a pain to do on the bus.

When my dad dropped me off, I realised just how little I really could see with the mask on. I couldn't see a thing. Everything was white because of the tint on the lenses, and they were steamed up. I smacked into a few poles, fences, walls, and doors on the way in. I called my mate Rob to come help me. He arrived and tried guiding me through the main hall. I walked into a piano, a row of chairs, and finally fell down some stairs. I am the worst Spider-Man ever. He eventually had to carry me to form.

I had an entire crowd of people following me. Spider-Man is not a common occurrence. Especially not around school, and especially not when he's being carried about because he just fell down some stairs. I finally arrived in form and Rob put me down. I had a crowd of people standing in the door asking for photos, autographs, and high fives. I had a lot of photos taken of me. I should have started charging £5 per photo. I would have made absolute bank.

We went out onto the field where there was a bouncy castle and a blow-up obstacle course. Perfect. I'm outside. I decided against letting the sex doll go in the sports hall and instead decided to let it go outside. I think it'd be funnier if a deflated sex doll ends up in someone's garden than in a sports hall. I had the sex doll and canister in a carrier bag that I then took behind science to fill up. I then let it go. It was funny to see it float off, but a bit underwhelming. I saw it get stuck in a tree on the way up but was soon blown back into the sky. That's my job done then. I do wonder where it'll land.

I went back to the blow-up obstacle course. My fat friend went on it, but it collapsed under his weight. The climbing wall bit crumpled like paper. What a sight to see!

Edward had brought in a big bag of shit he bought from a charity shop. He had a magic wand. He went round using it to cast spells on people and giving them AIDS. That isn't exactly what I'd do if I had a magic wand, but hey, each to his own. Maybe it was an AIDS wand where the only spell gives people AIDS. You never know.

We then had an assembly. I was the only one dressed up, so it was a bit weird. We got the results for who won the things like "Best couple", or "Most likely to be a comedian". I was nominated for the comedian one but didn't win. Believe it or not, it was one of the popular kids that won because it's the students that vote. You could be the funniest bloke in the world, but it wouldn't matter because he got all his mates to vote for him. Bullshit. I'm absolutely hilarious.

I went into town after school. I was still dressed as Spider-Man. I saw a young boy that looked no older than 10 and was wearing a Spider-Man T-shirt and Spider-Man hat. He saw me and I just saw his eyes widen. He tapped his mum on the arm and pointed at me. I waved at him, and I could see him smiling. I bet that made his day. Spider-Man waved at him. I guess to him and all the other kids at school who wanted photos, I **was** Spider-Man. Not just some autistic idiot.

I then went home to get ready for prom. My brother gave me a hip flask of vodka to help give me confidence. I knew I'd have no chance in asking Grace to dance with me otherwise. With my hip flask and suit, I left for prom certain it'd go well.

I arrived. I then saw what one of the popular kids came in. A tank. A fucking tank. Someone had hired a tank to take them to prom. I'd seen a few girls arrive in a limo, but... a tank?! Show-off. My mum drove me.

I found Edward. He was actually wearing a suit. He looks weird with a suit. I then looked at the tie he was wearing. It was a Winnie-the-Pooh tie. Typical. There were a bunch of drinks on a table in the middle of the room. They all had mint leaves in them. Edward said, *"What jackass put leaves in all the drinks?"* I couldn't be bothered arguing with him.

Some of the girls look fucking weird. They have these large dresses that look like they got them form a Disney shop. They looked like they were cosplaying Cinderella. There were weirder clothing choices though. The goth people were dressed like time travellers, and I saw one guy dressed like Elton John. I saw another guy dressed like Jimi Hendrix; he was wearing an all-orange suit with a flowery shirt. He hadn't ironed his trousers though, because I could see crease marks all over his legs and crotch.

I saw Grace walk in. She looked beautiful. She was wearing a slim blue dress and had lovely hair.

Everyone then sat down for dinner. There was confetti scattered on the tables. Edward thought they were stickers and was trying to peel the back off them and stick them to his shirt. It didn't work.

The first course was soup. Edward said he hated it and that it tasted like vomit. I told him to just eat the bread that came with it then. He asked me to hand him the plate of butter in the middle of the table. I did. He scraped a big bit of butter off with his knife. I thought he was going to scrape it on his bread, but no, he just ate it. He just ate an entire chunk of butter. Fuck me he's an idiot.

Edward then called his mum. He then didn't say goodbye and forgot to hang up, so he put the phone in his pocket while still on the phone to his mum. I think that takes the cake. I honestly have no idea how he has survived to this age.

After we had all eaten our food, they started playing music. I went up to the dance floor and tried to show off my moves to impress Grace. I tried doing the moonwalk. It didn't work though, so it just looked like I was walking backwards. I should've practiced more.

Everyone then got up and started dancing. Grace included. She was with her friends though, so I waited a bit for her to sort of move away from them. I thought *"This is my chance!"* I started walking towards her. She looked at me and walked away and I lost her in the crowd. Some of my friends were still sat down at the tables, so I went and sat down with them. I explained I was having a hard time getting the opportunity to ask her. I didn't want to pull her away from her friends and I couldn't get a hold of her on her own because she walks off. I thought I'd try one last time. I started to approach her, but she simply walked off and disappeared again. *"That's it"* I thought. I went and sat down at a separate table. I took a glass off the table and pulled out the hip flask from my inner jacket pocket. I put the glass under the table and poured some vodka into it. I tried diluting it with some water, but they only had fizzy water. Bad idea. Don't drink fizzy vodka.

I was still feeling sober, so I thought I'd screw diluting it and just drink it pure. I poured it into the glass under the table. That's when I heard *"I'll be taking that."* I looked up to see a teacher standing beside me with an outstretched hand. At that moment, I felt my brain go numb. I had no idea what to do. I can't be seen with this! I tried pleading with him by saying it's only water. He said, *"Let's have a taste then."* I tried pouring the rest on the floor before I gave it to him. I then handed it to him. He tried the few drops that were left and said, *"No, that tastes like vodka to me. Let's take a walk, shall we?"* I felt my heart sink and my soul leave my body. I reluctantly stood up and followed him through the room. He was holding the flask in a way as though he was making sure everyone could see what I'd done. Everyone watched me walk out. Everyone saw the flask. Everyone knows. The teacher led me to a room where all the other teachers were. I saw the headmaster, the deputy head, all of them. I explained I only did it because I had no confidence and wanted to ask a girl to dance with me. It was then that I started crying.

I went home too drunk to process it all. I took my suit off and scrunched it up and left it a heap on the floor.

I never did get my dance with Grace in the end.

Saturday 7th May 2022

Well shit.

I woke up sober enough to understand what happened. My Spider-Man costume was folded neatly on my chair and my suit was a crumpled mess, carelessly thrown on the floor. I felt rubbish and I had a headache.

I went downstairs to get a cup of tea. I was the only one in the house because my parents went out somewhere.

I don't know what else to write, so I thought I'd end with a poem.

> *"I was stupid for having hopes that don't match my capabilities*
> *I had my head in the clouds looking at the possibilities*
> *Like in an aquarium gazing at exotic fish*
> *Too busy looking in awe; that's how I didn't get my wish*
> *If I had the confidence, alcohol wouldn't have been needed*
> *In the end, "It's only water" is what I pleaded*
> *I guess I paid the price for my stupidity, but there's always tomorrow*
> *No point in looking back on yesterday's sorrow*
> *I think I'll throw in the towel for now though."*

And one final note: I learnt a valuable lesson today. I don't think I'll pursue Grace anymore. There is a famous quote: *"Don't look for happiness in the same place you lost it."* I don't think it's worth the fuss and I'm fucking knackered.

Printed in Great Britain
by Amazon

82913067R00078